AF400904

Every Colour
by Itself

Every Colour by Itself

Francis Upritchard

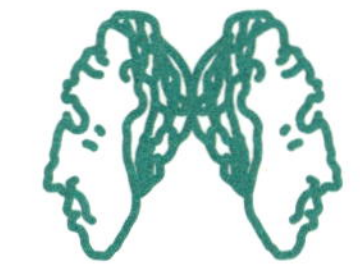

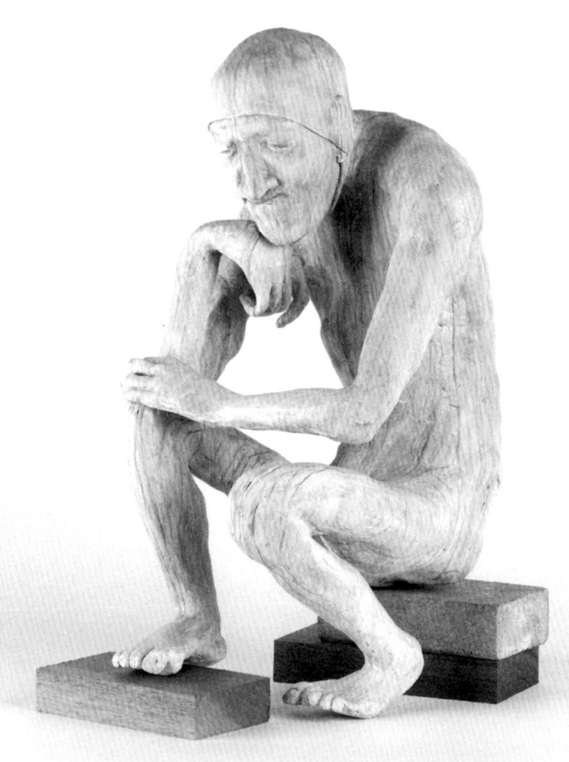

1

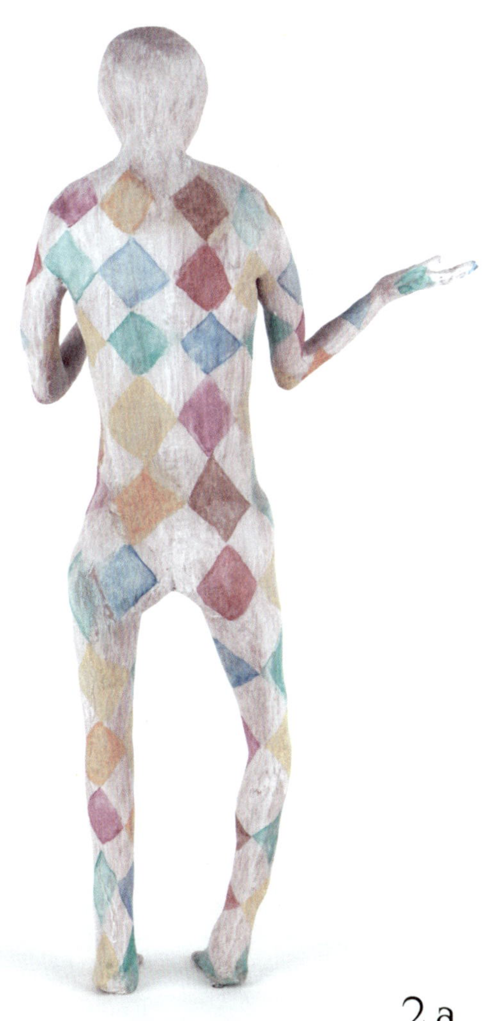

2 a

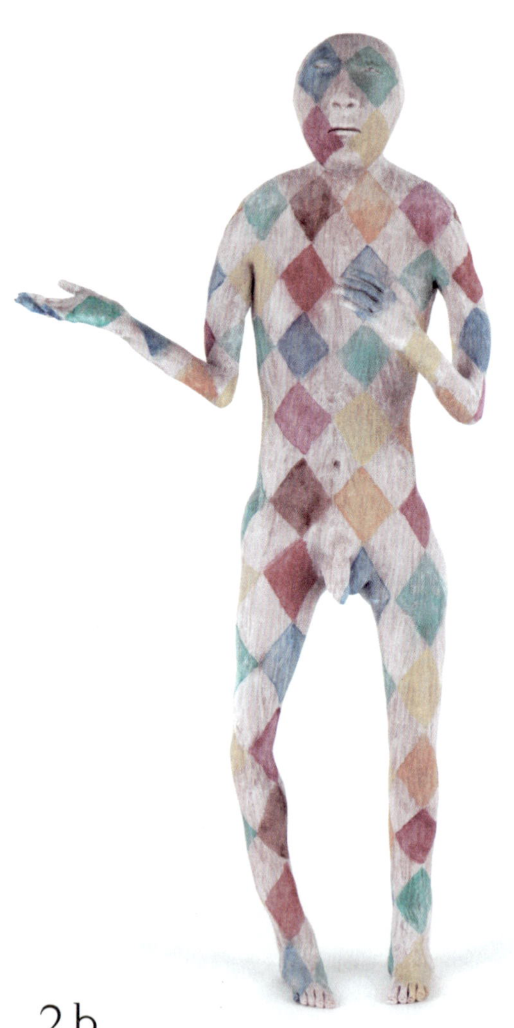

2 b

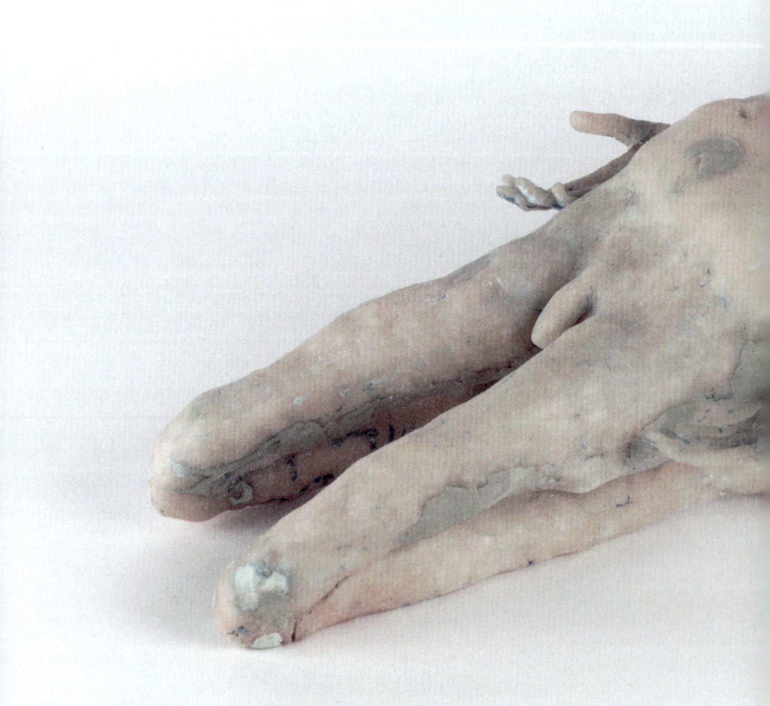

3 a

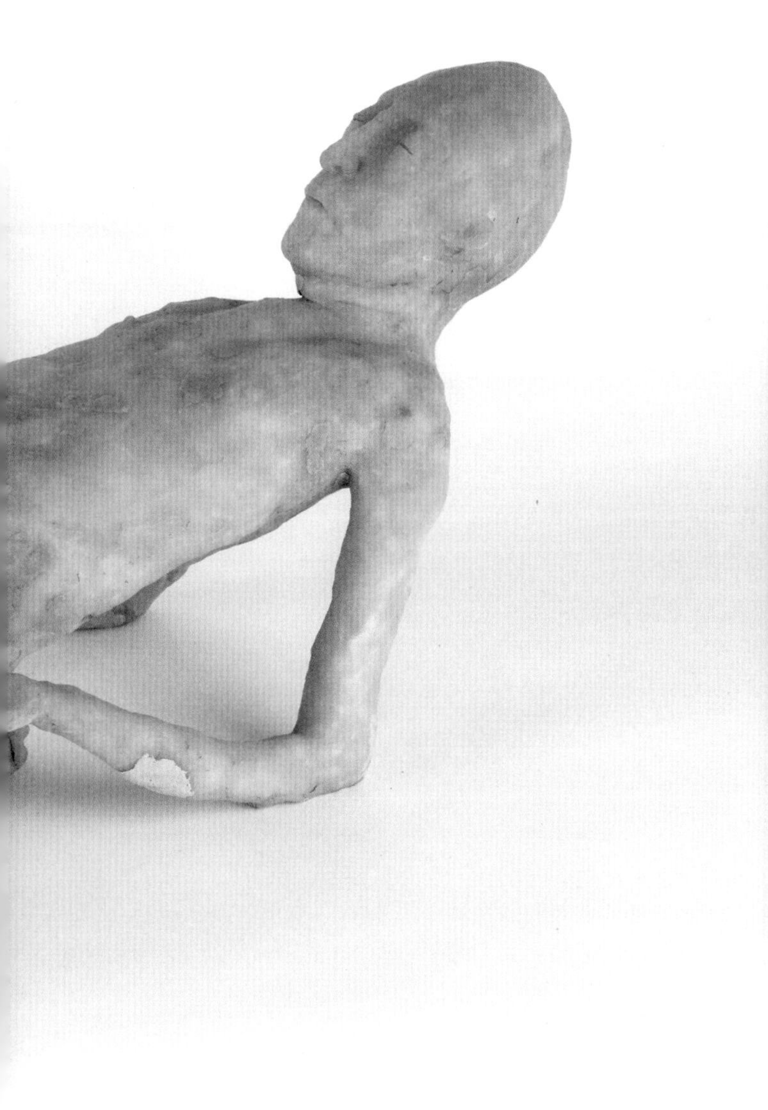

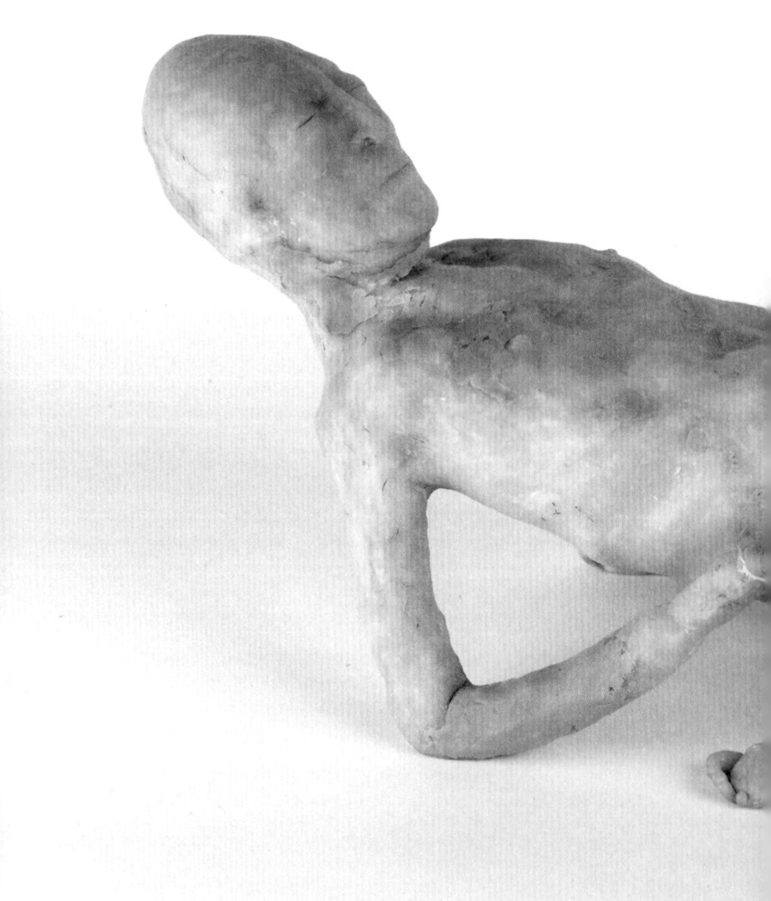

3 a

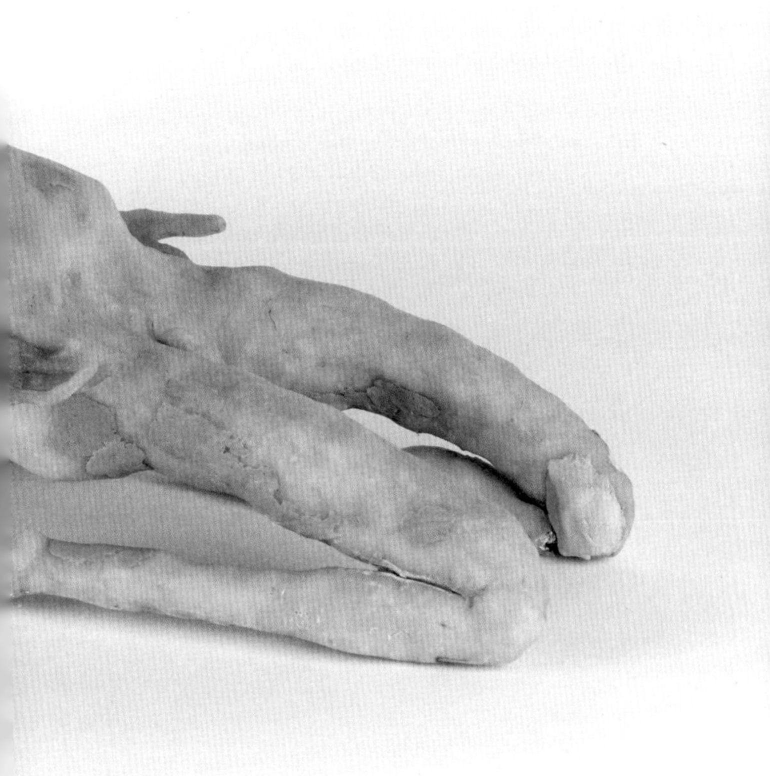

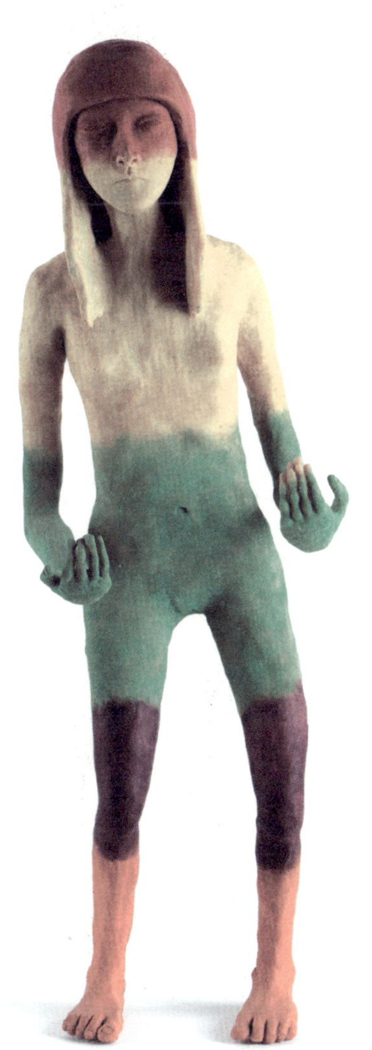

4 a

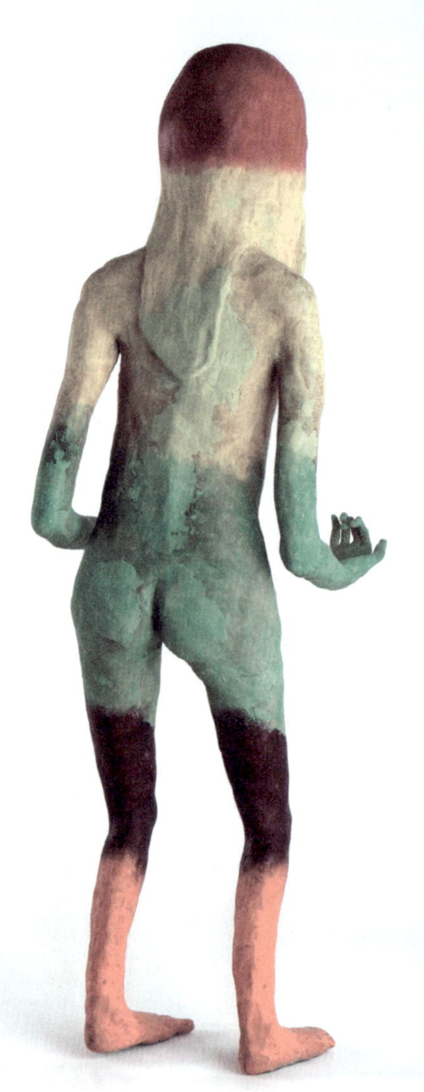

4 b

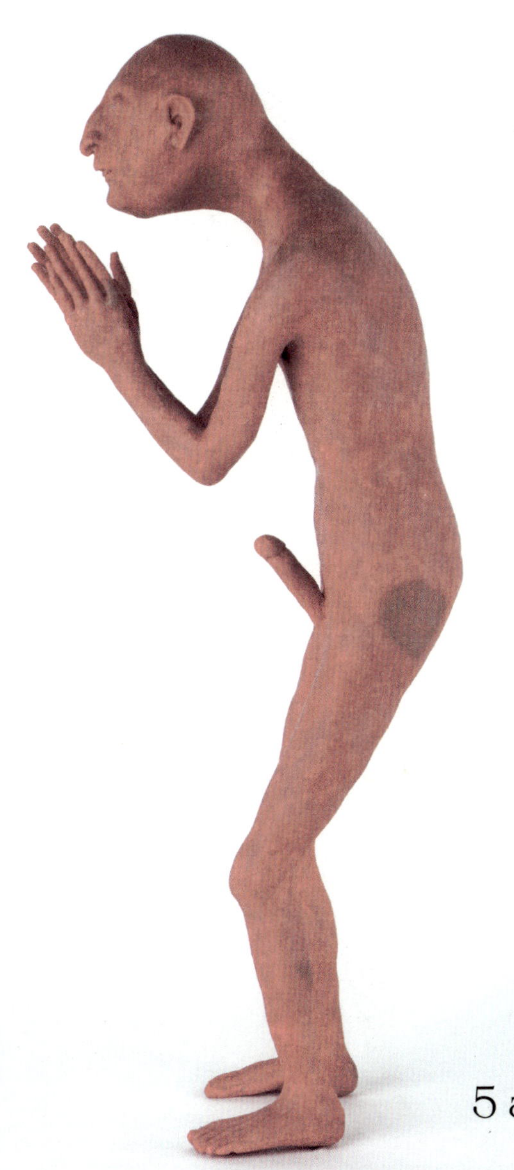

5 a

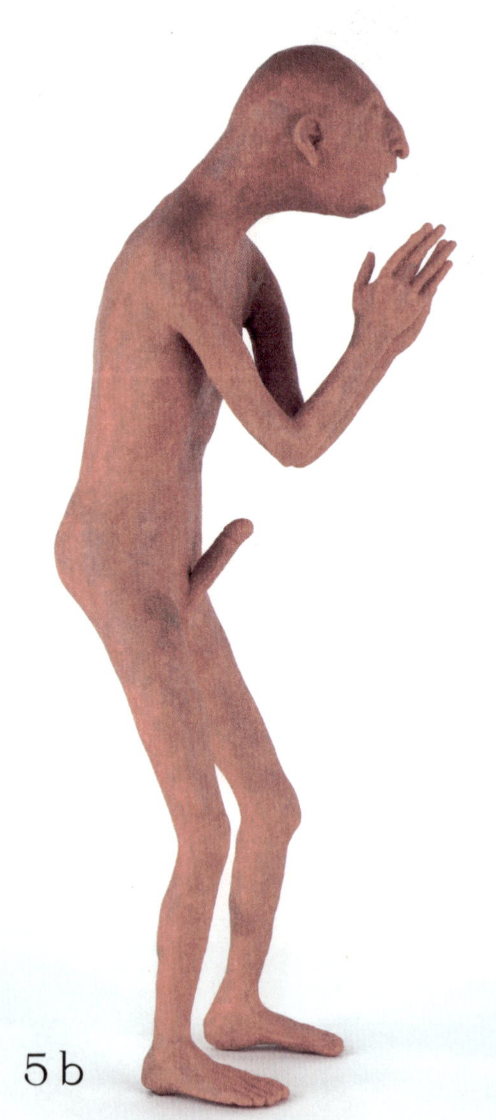

5 b

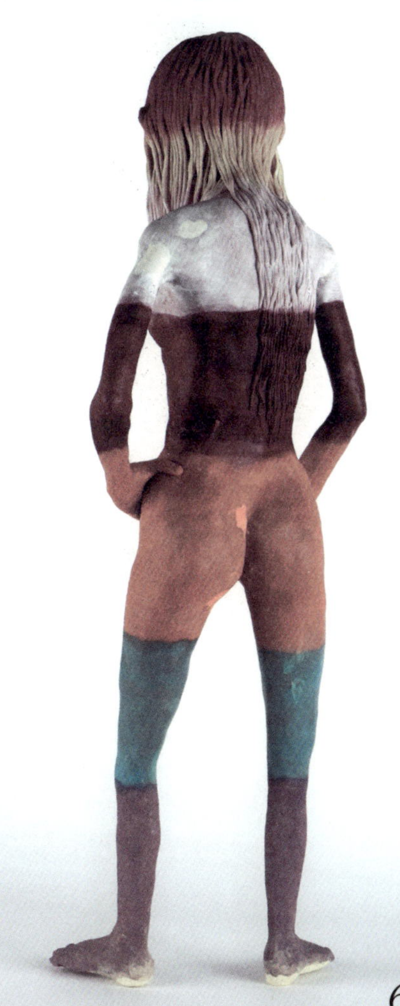

6 a

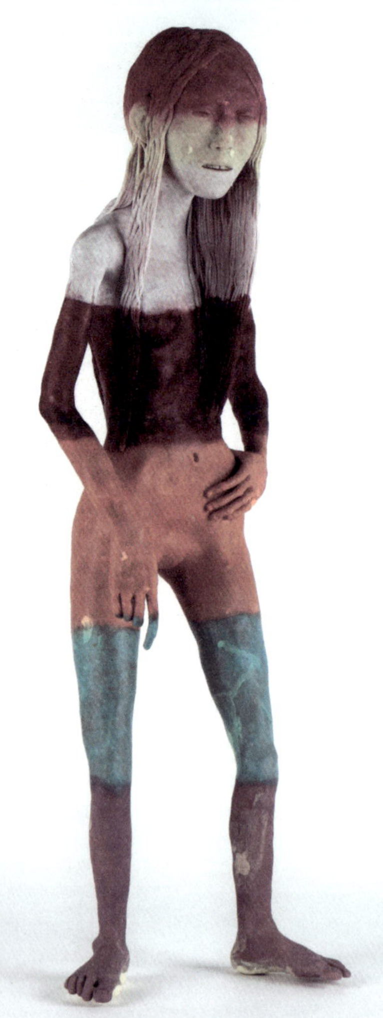

6 b

7

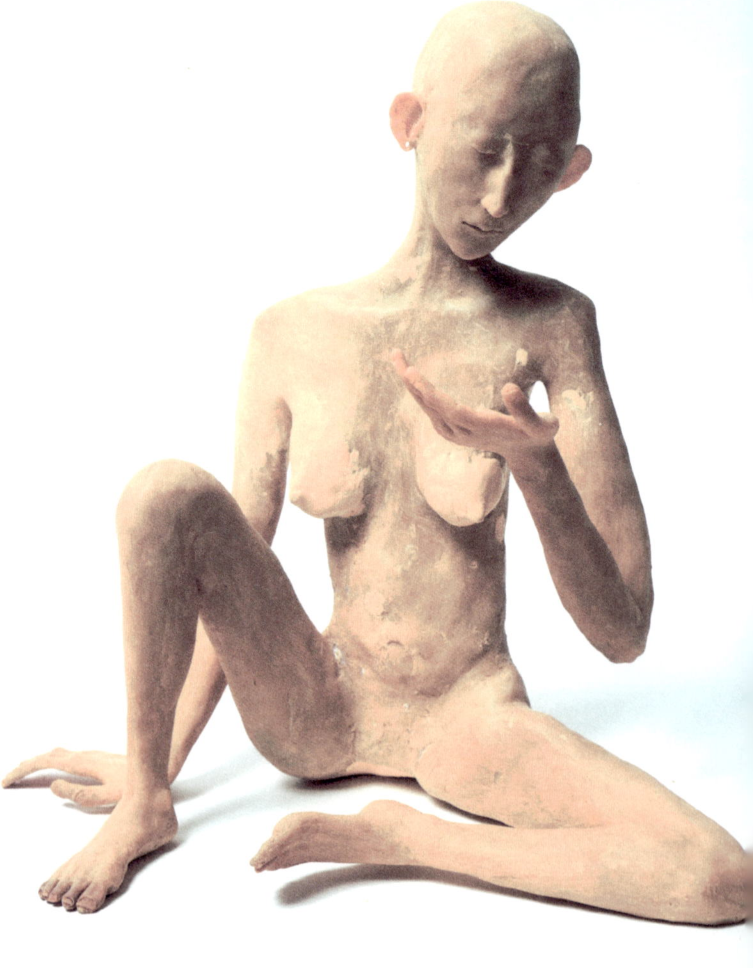

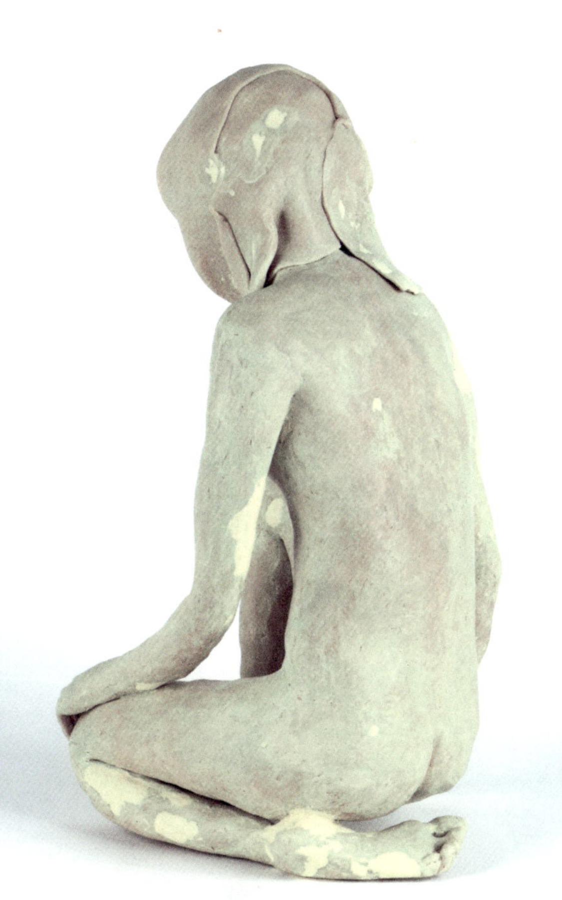

8 a

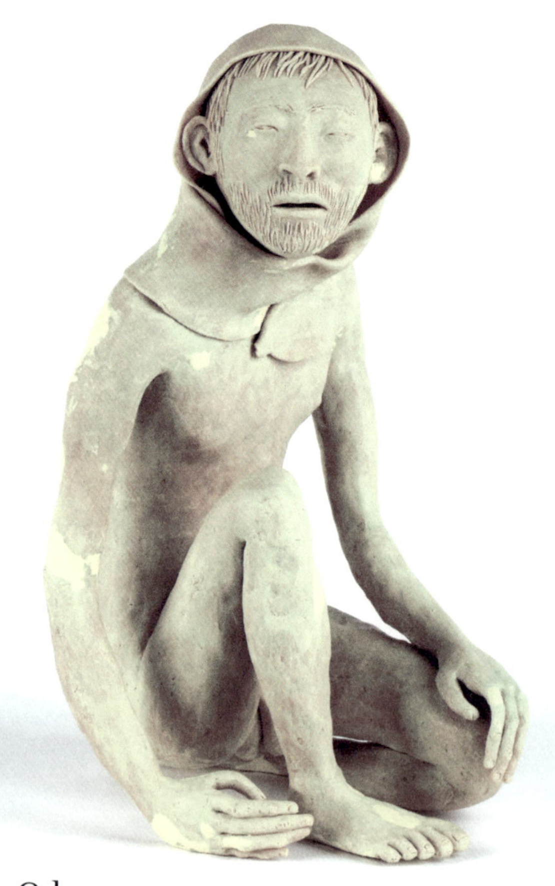

8 b

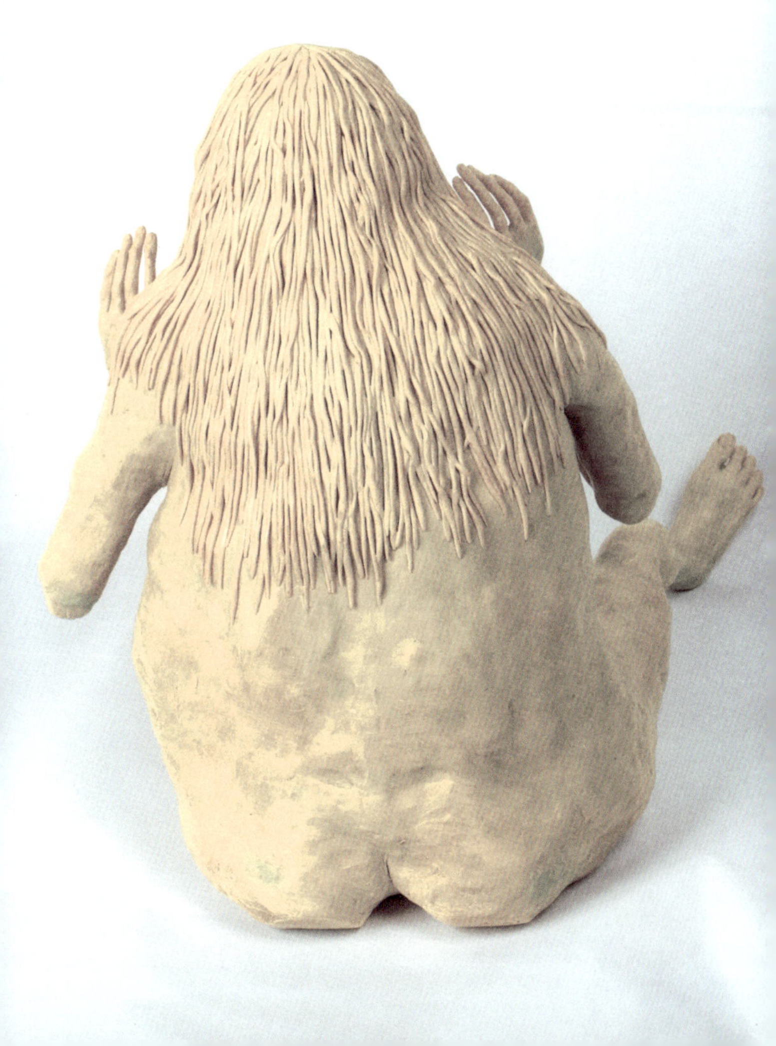

9 a

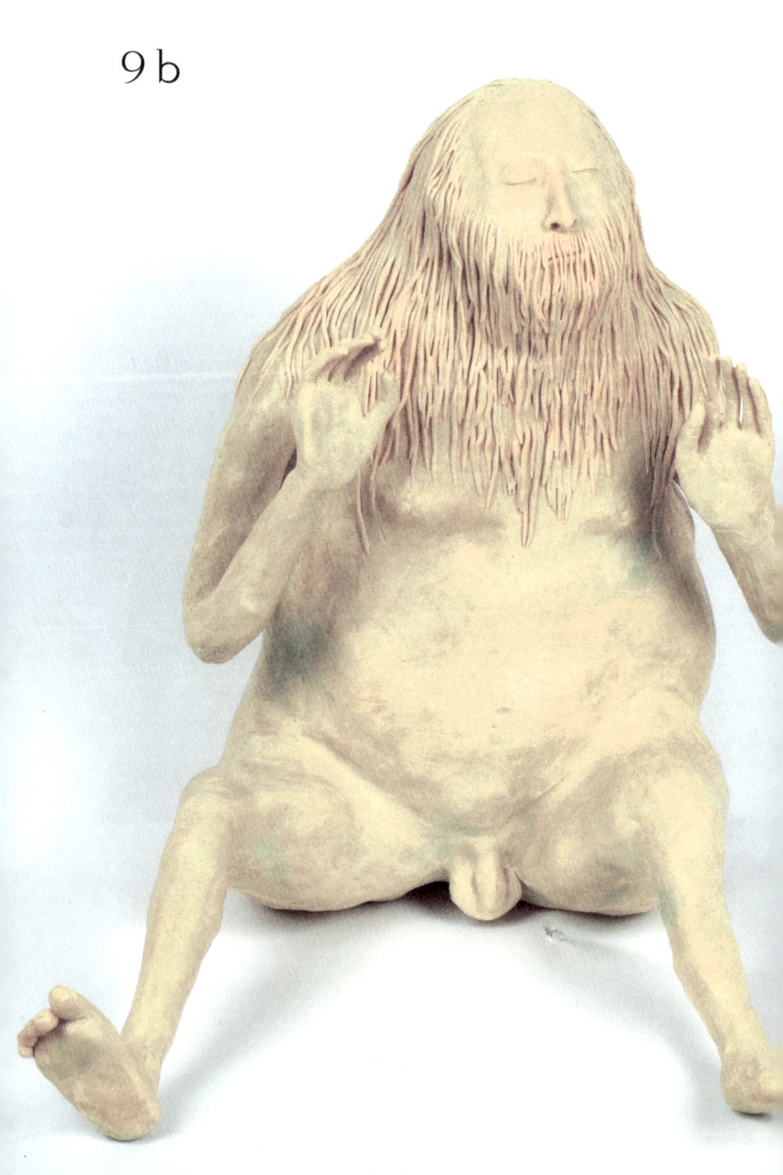

9b

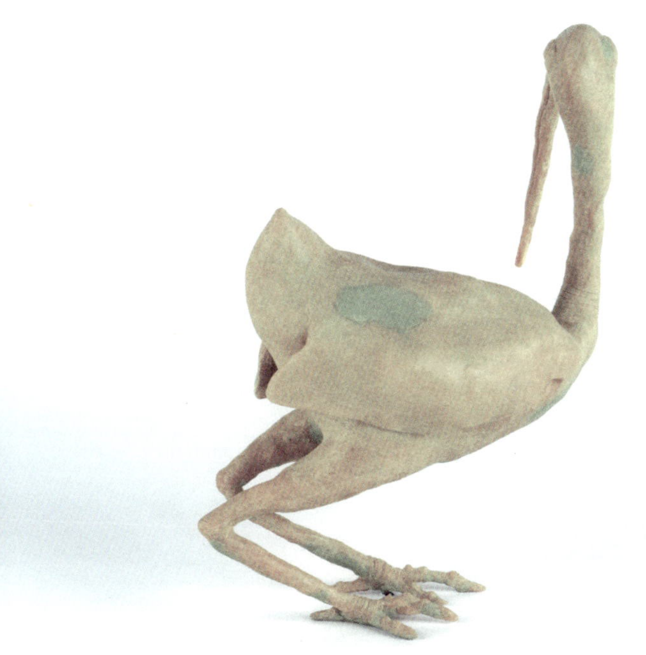

10 a

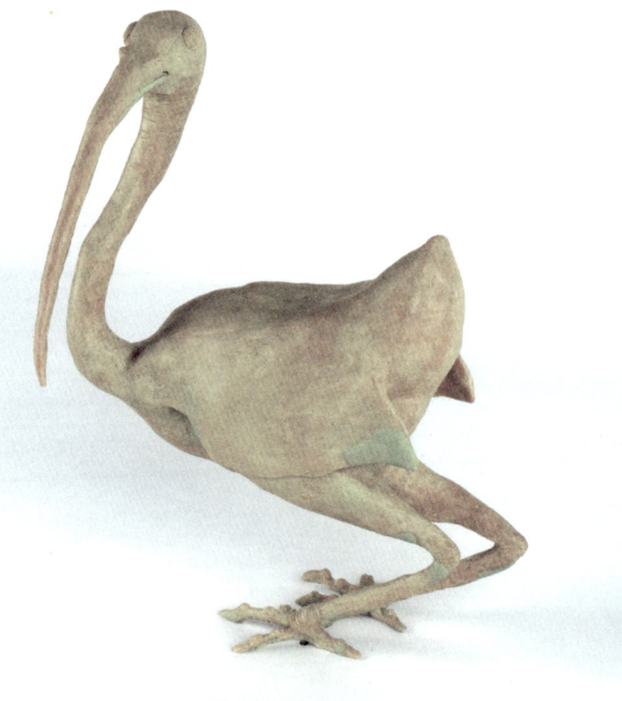

10 b

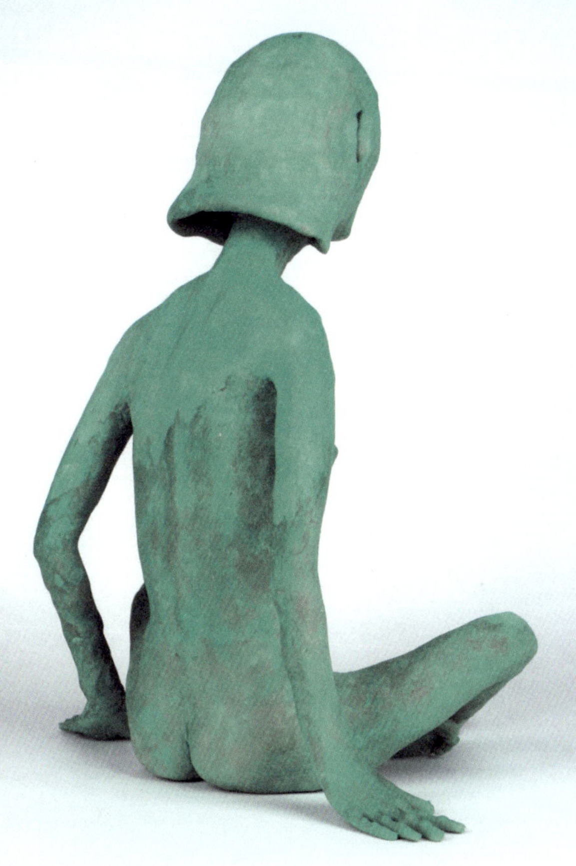

11 a

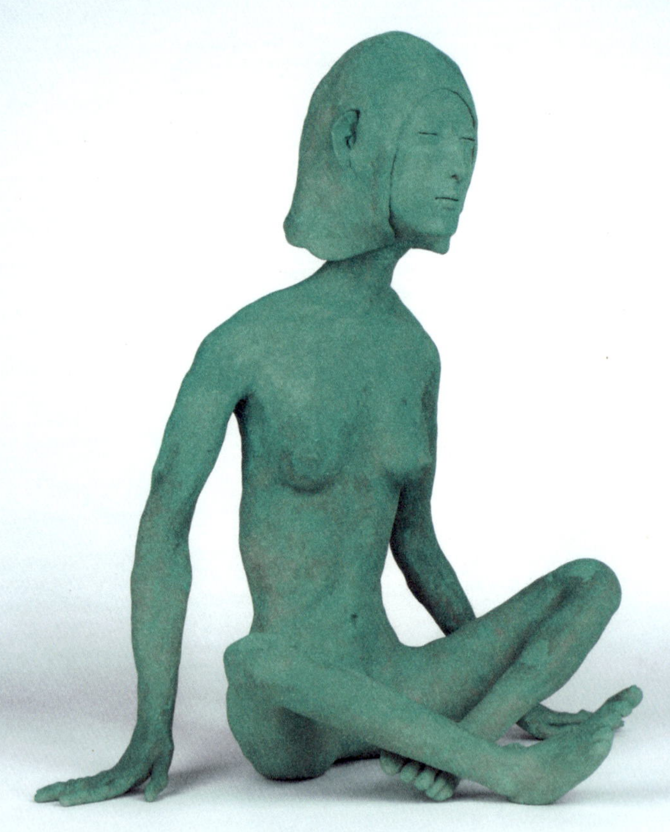

11 b

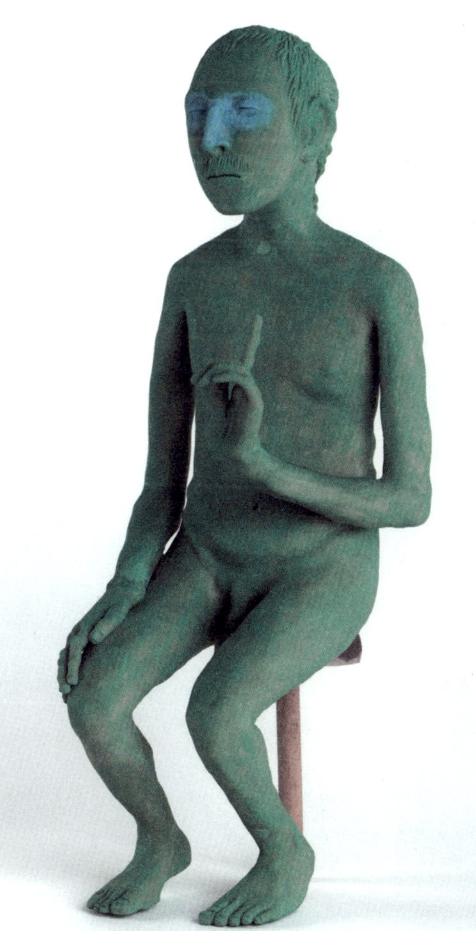

12 a

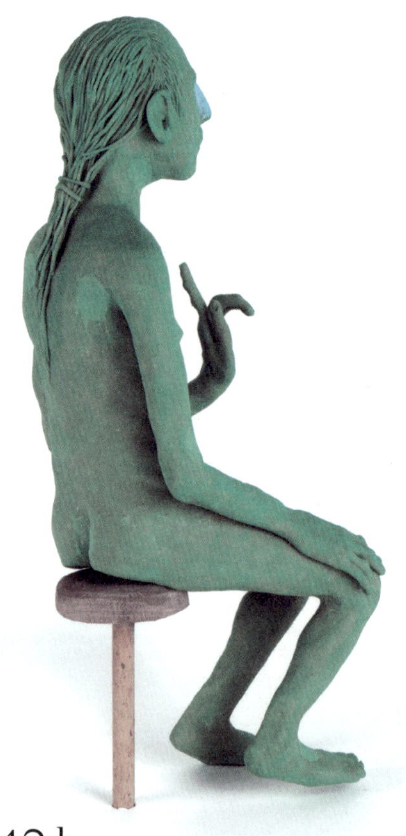

12 b

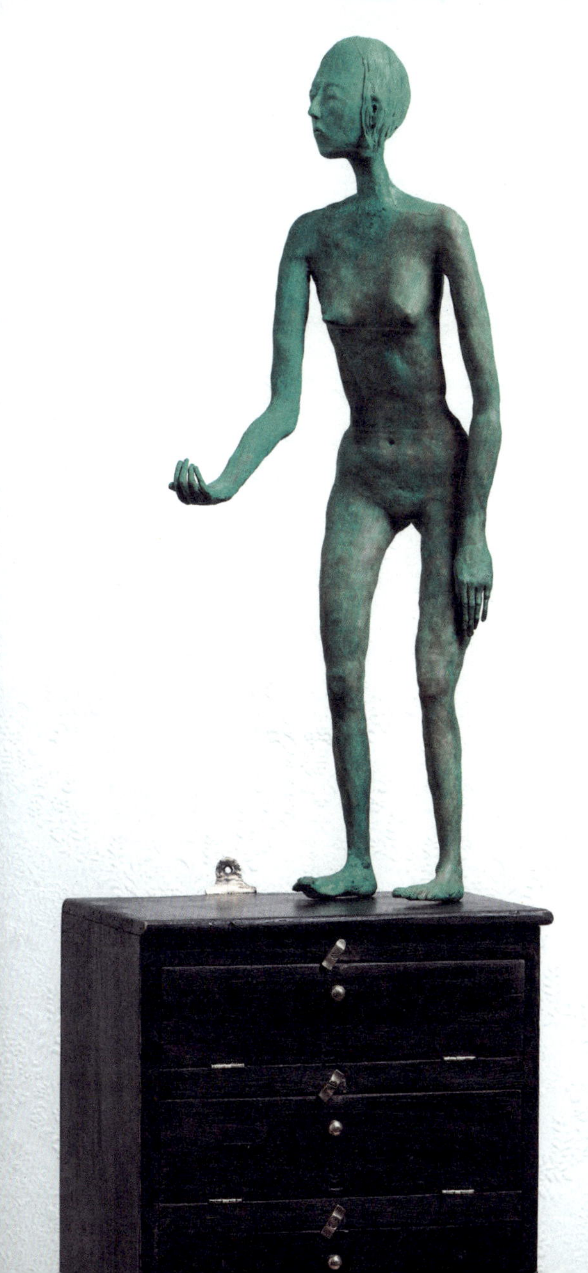

13

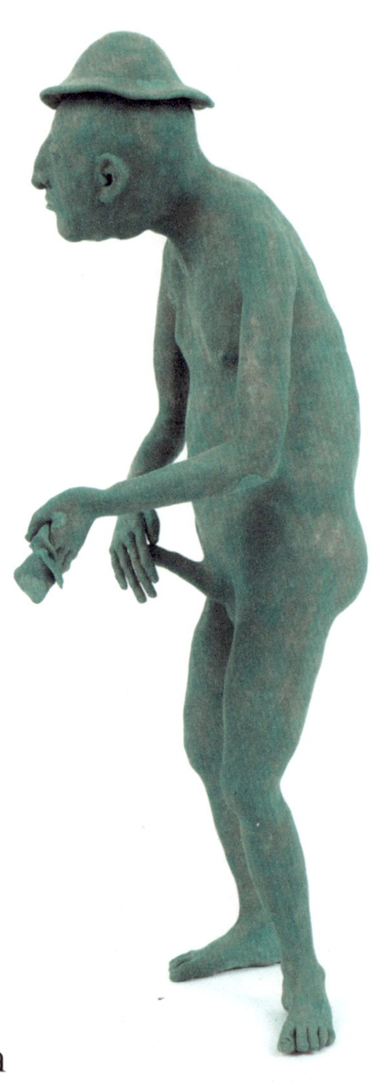

14 a

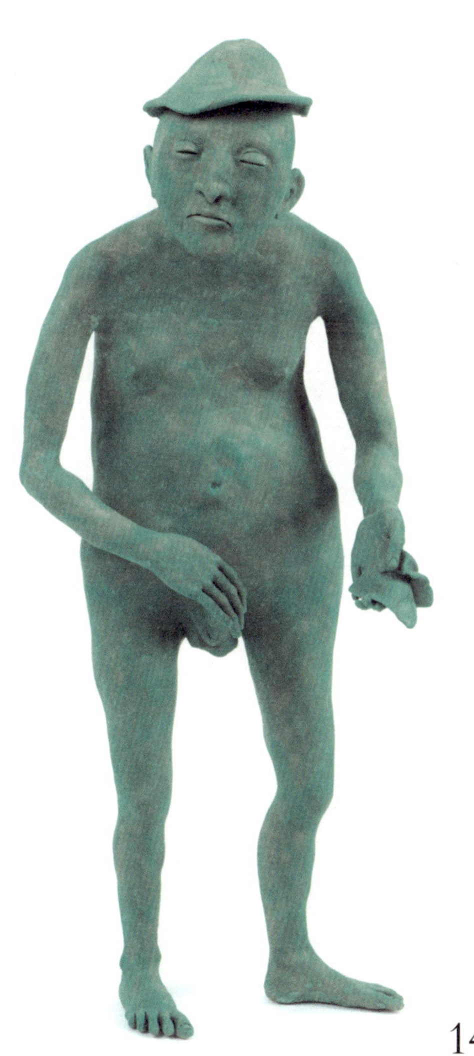

14 b

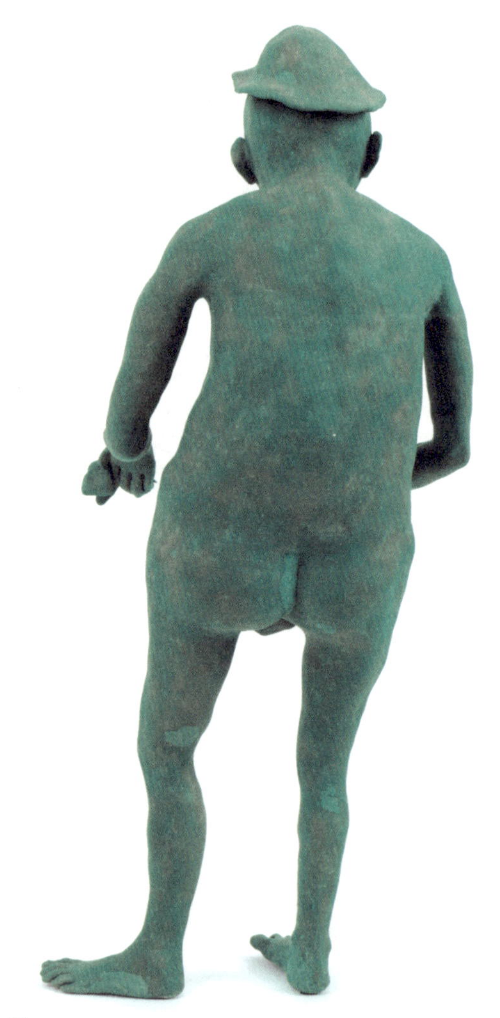

14 c

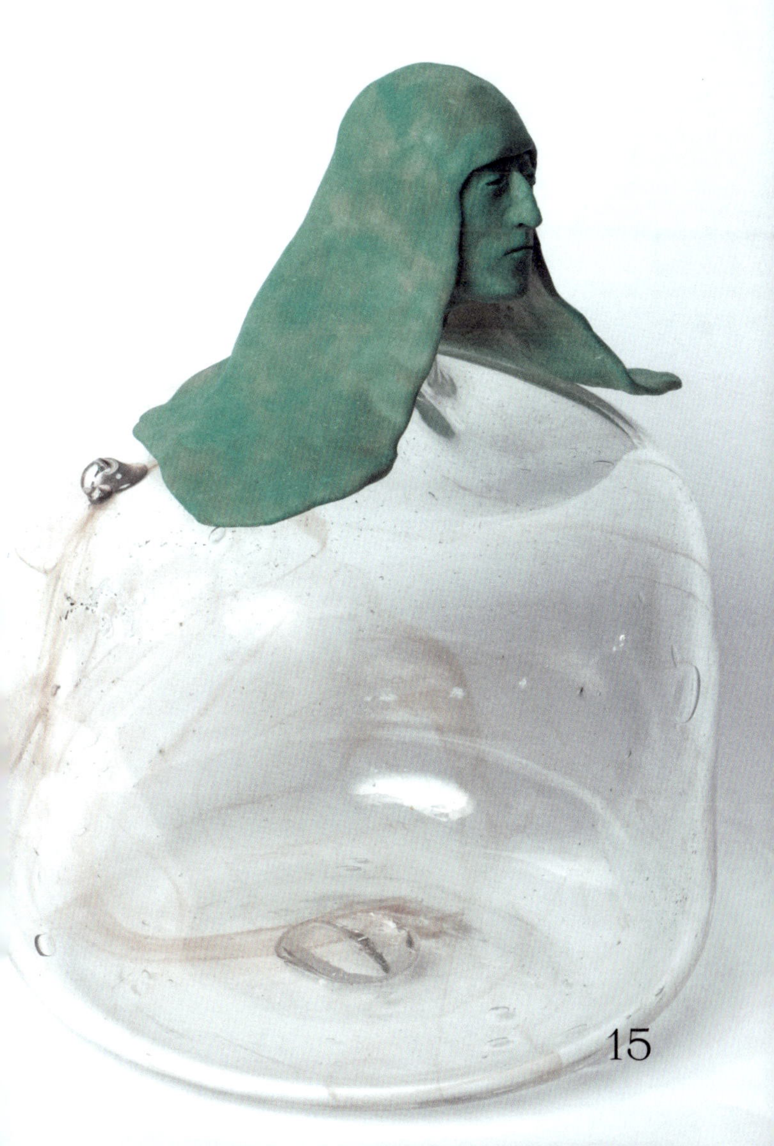

15

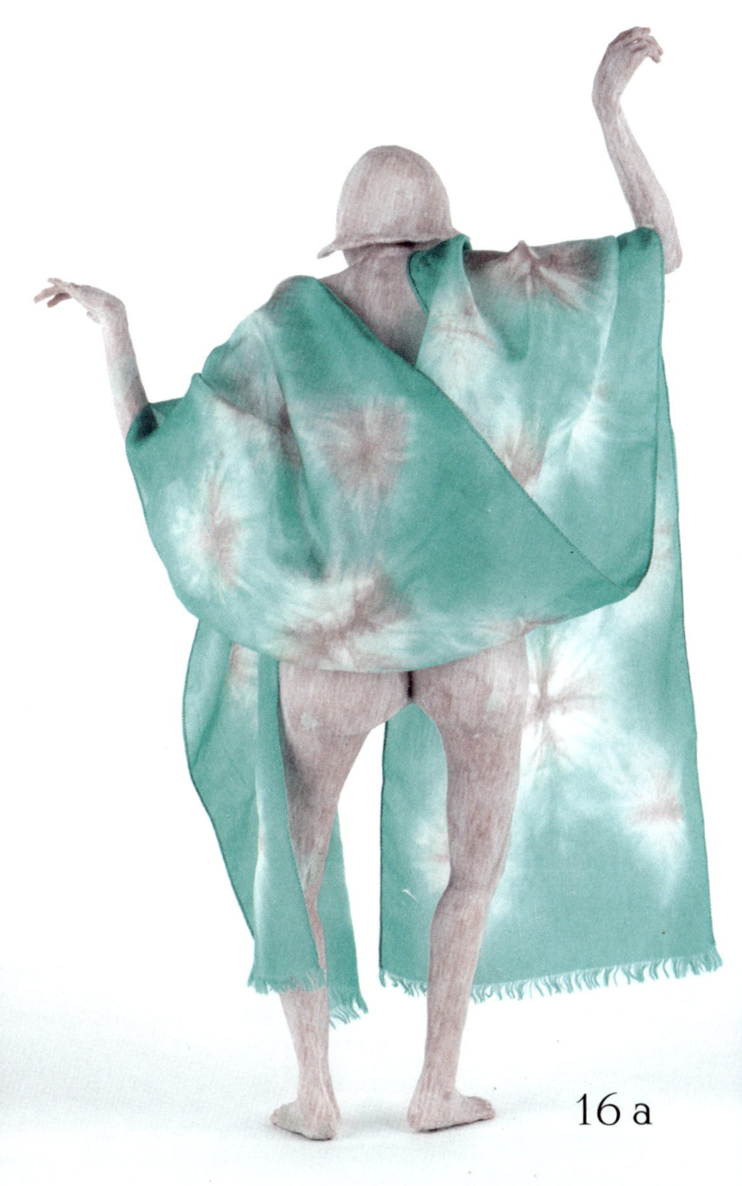

16 a

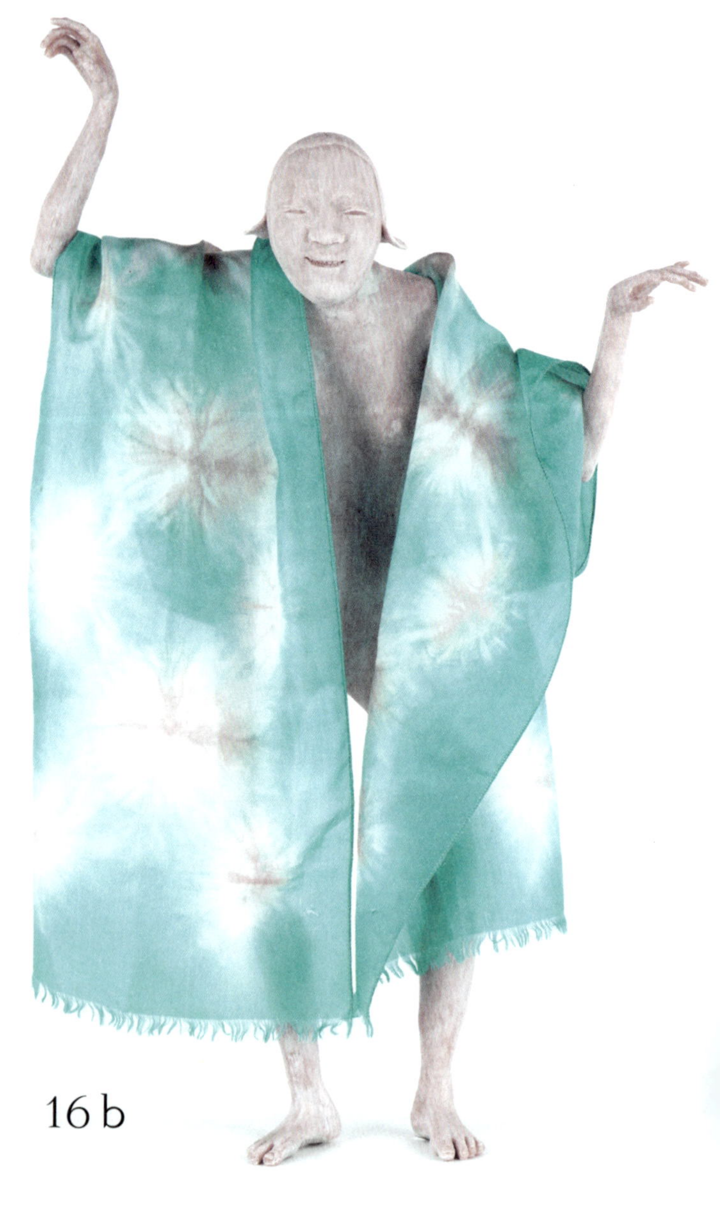

16 b

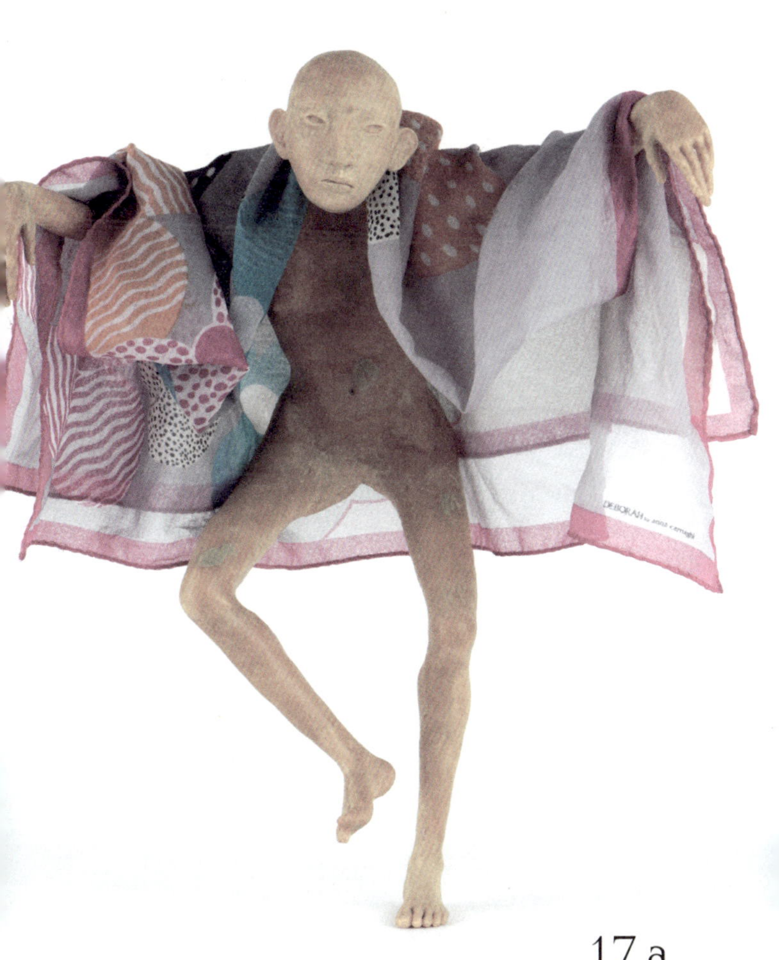

17 a

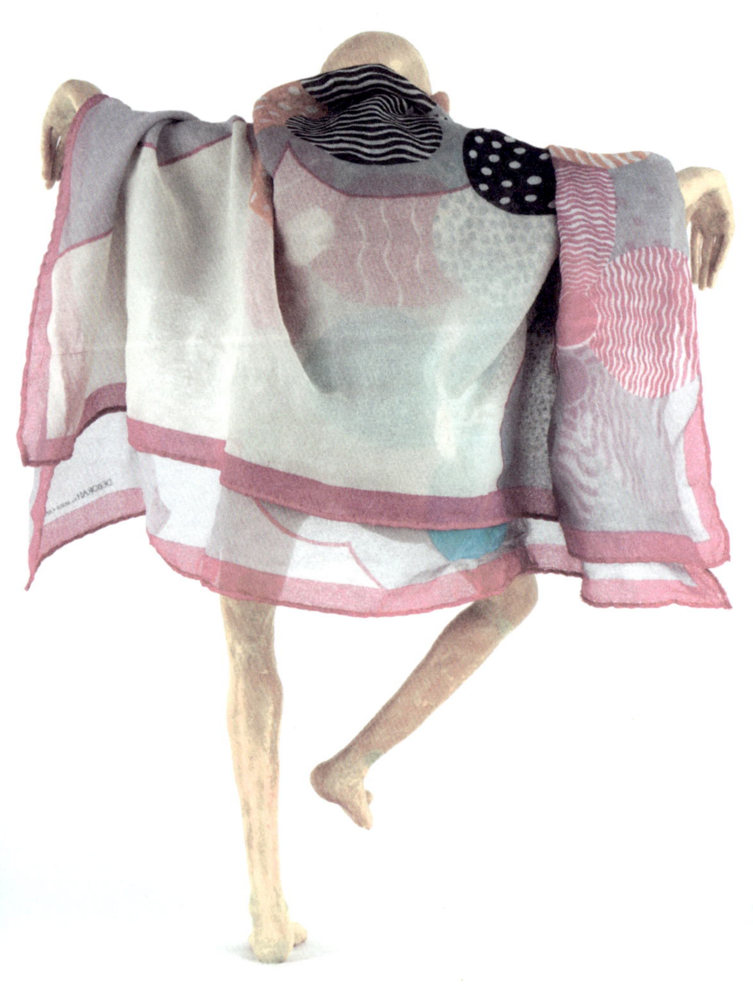

17 b

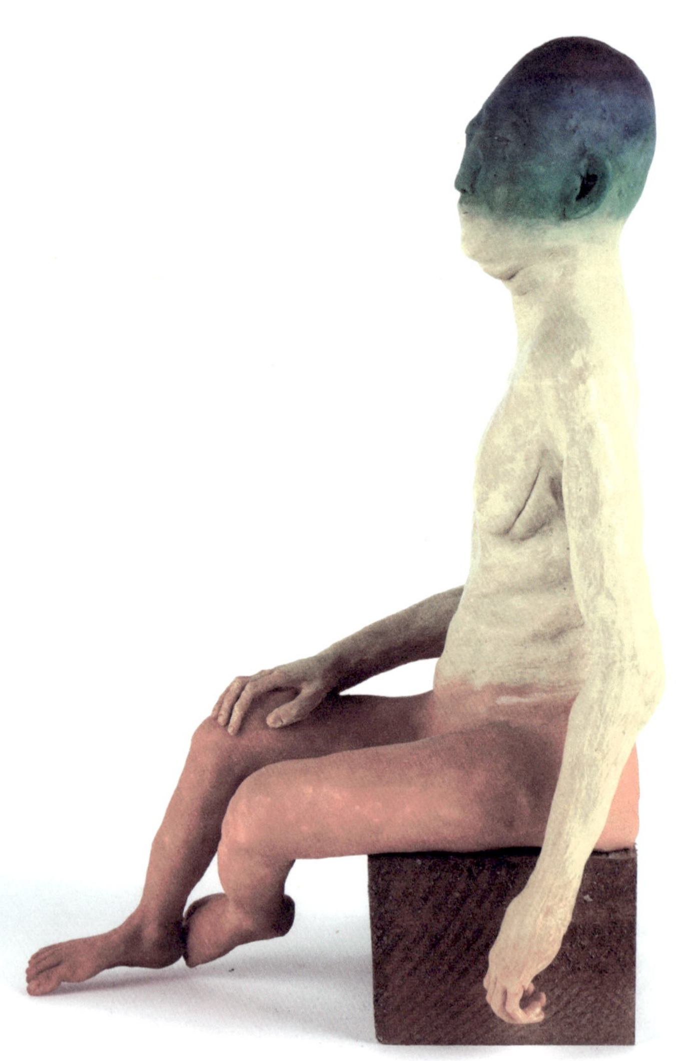

18 a

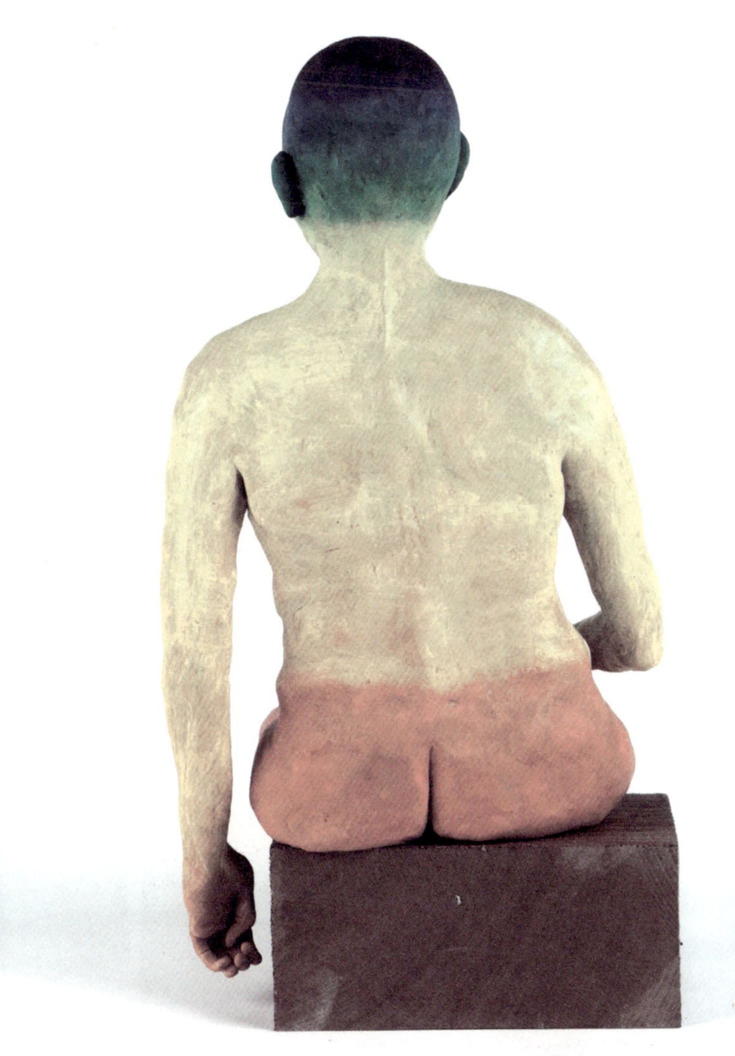

18 b

18 c

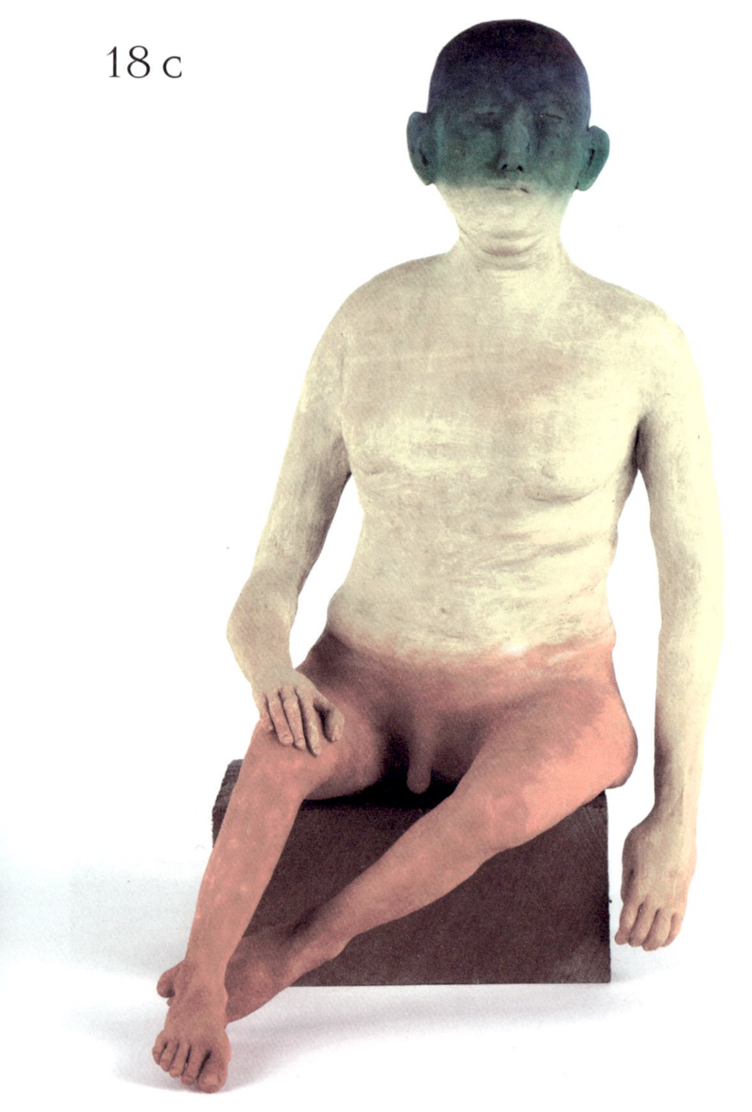

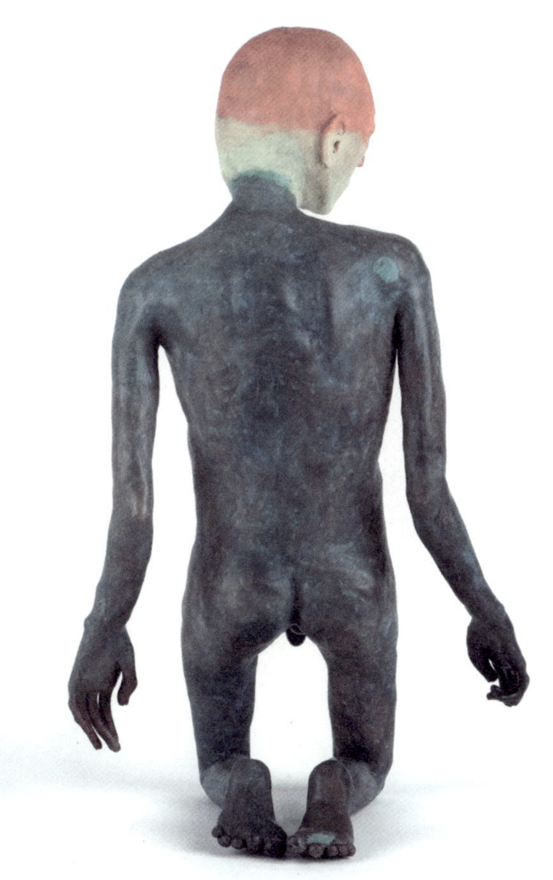

19 a

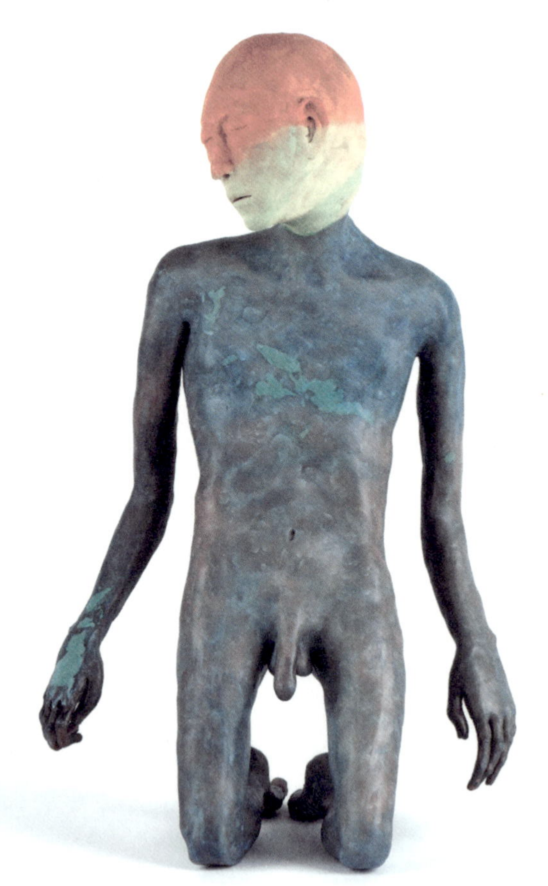

19 b

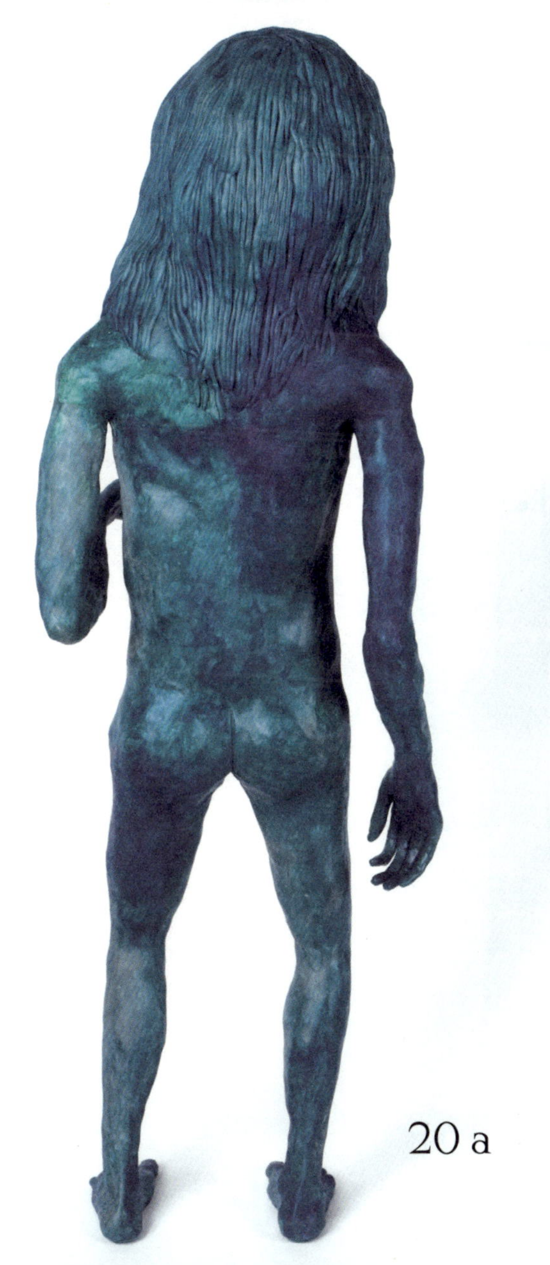

20 a

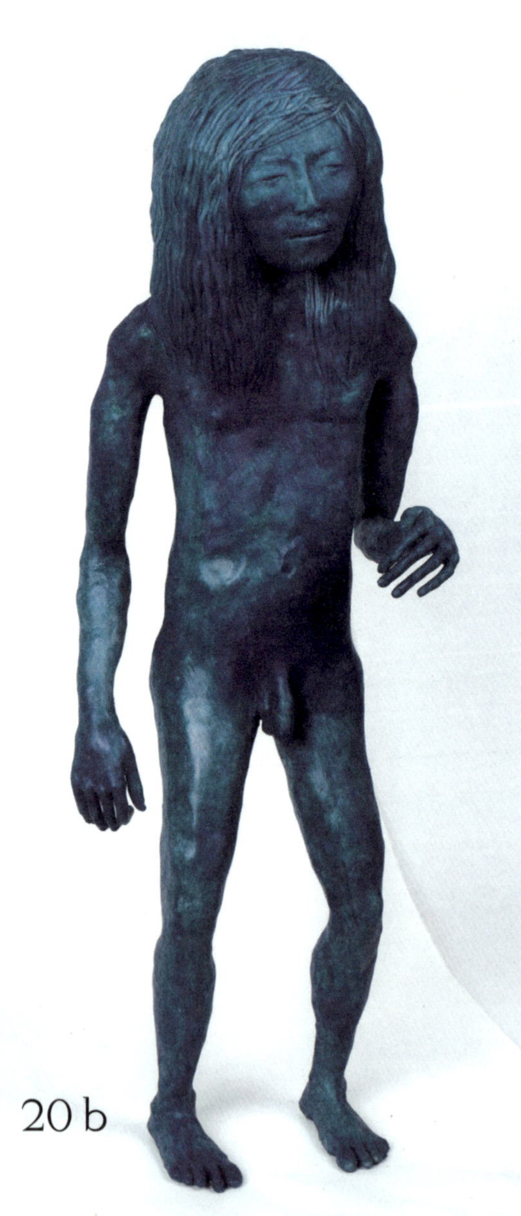

20 b

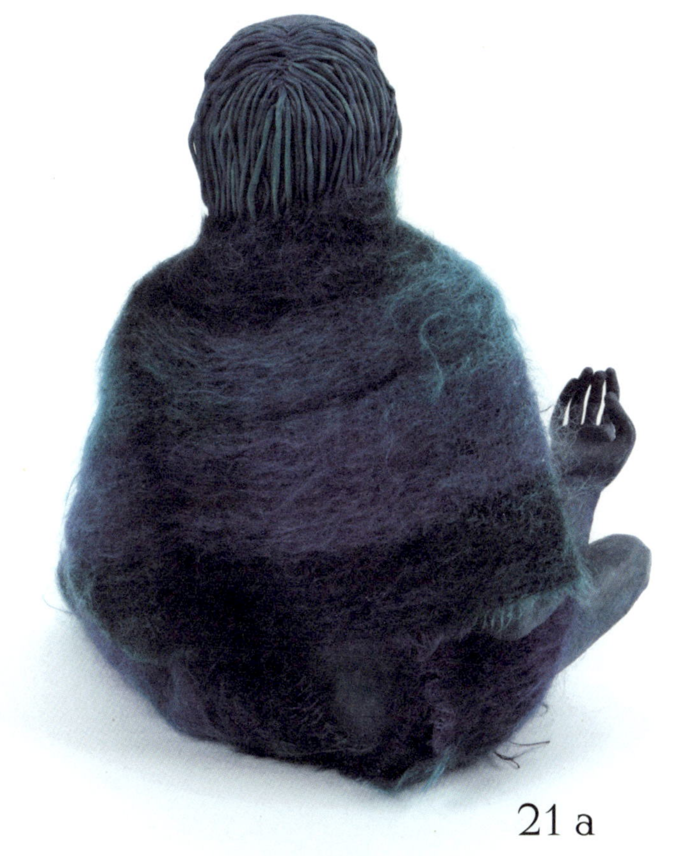

21 a

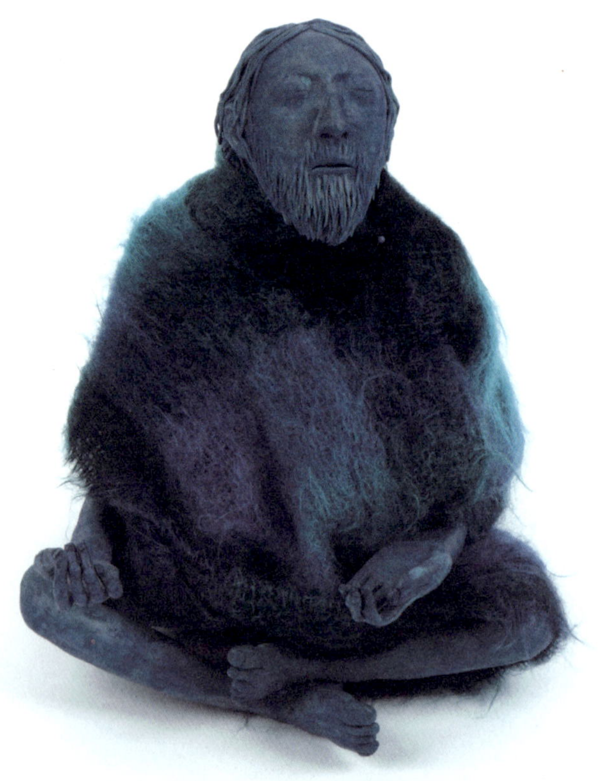

21 b

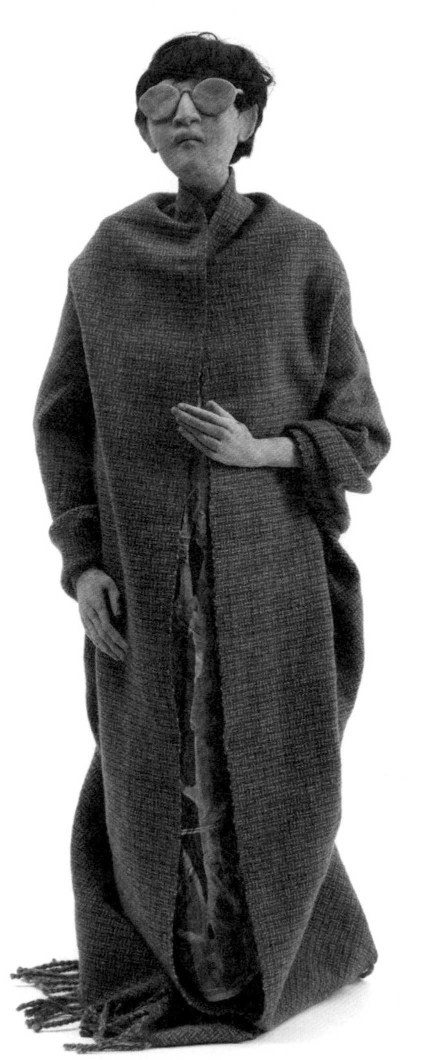

22

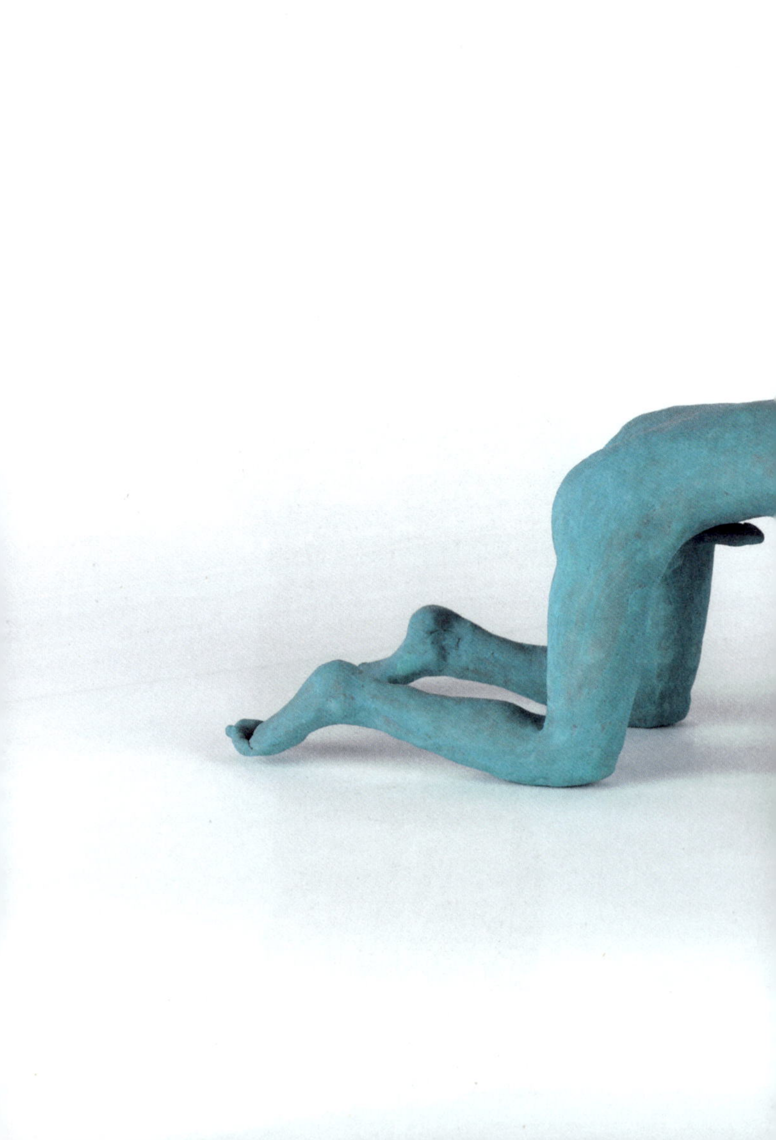

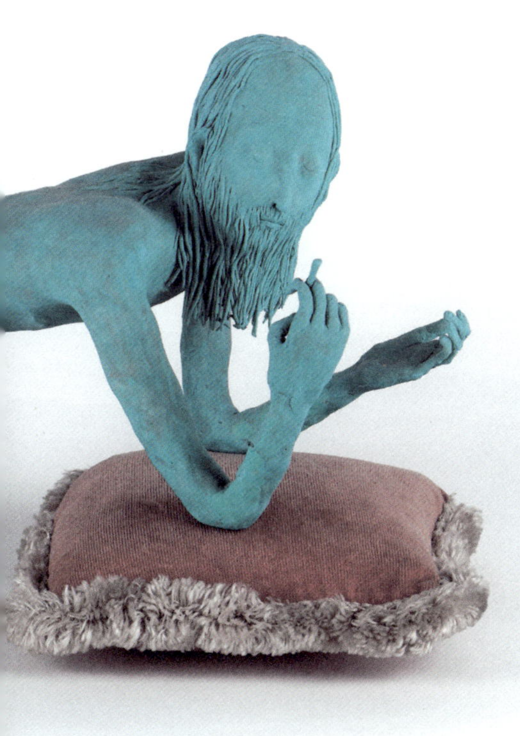

23

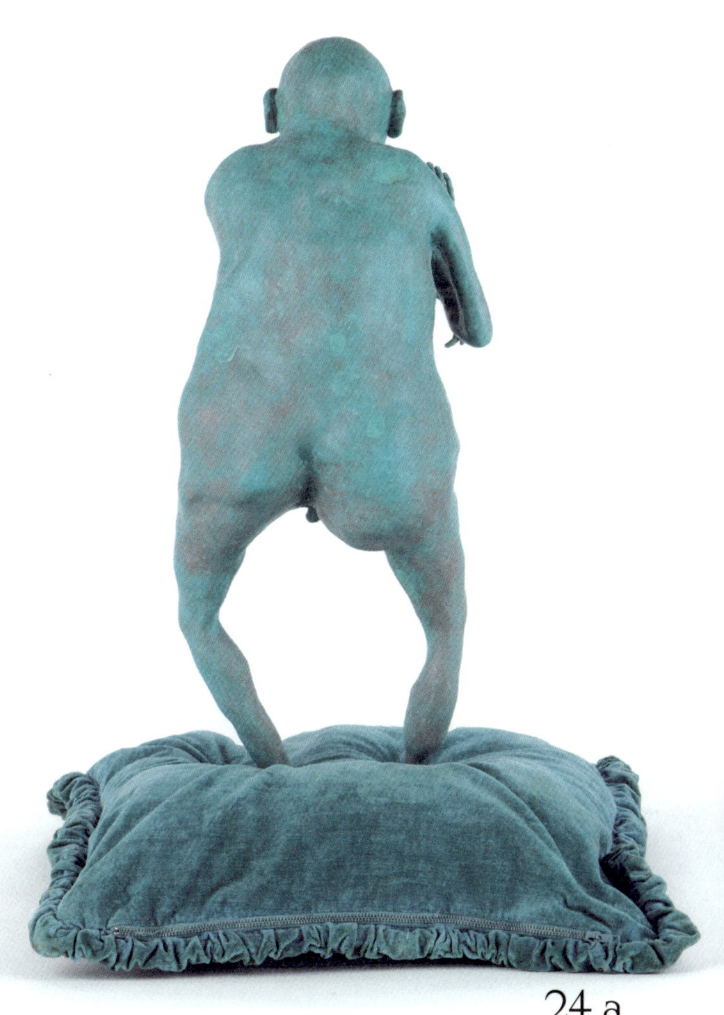

24 a

24 b

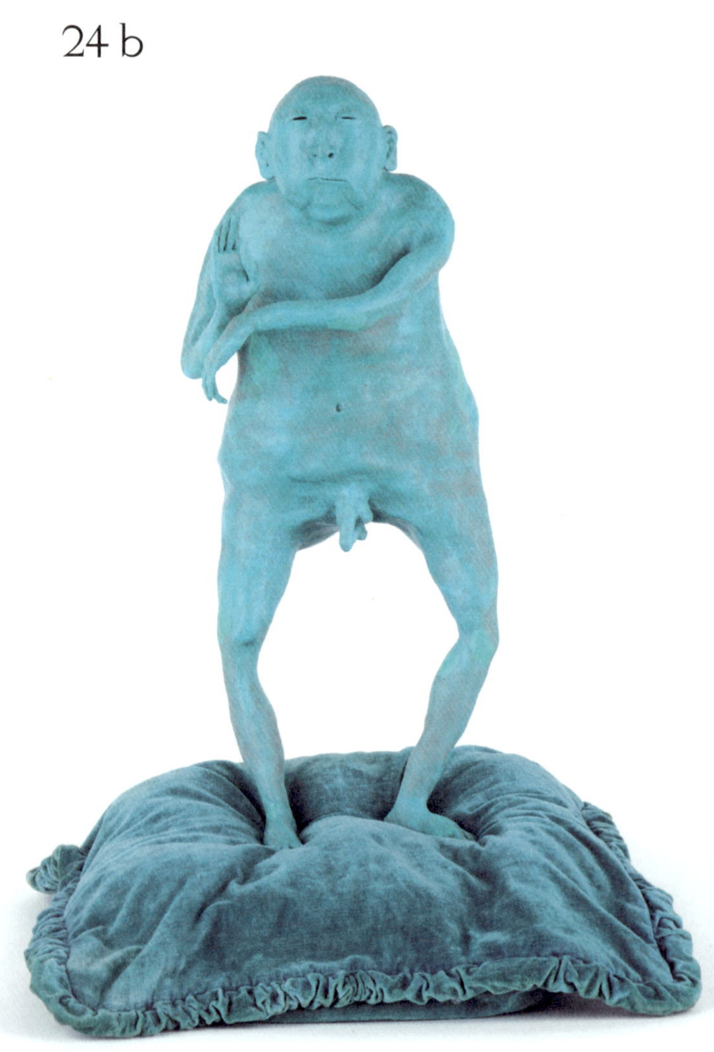

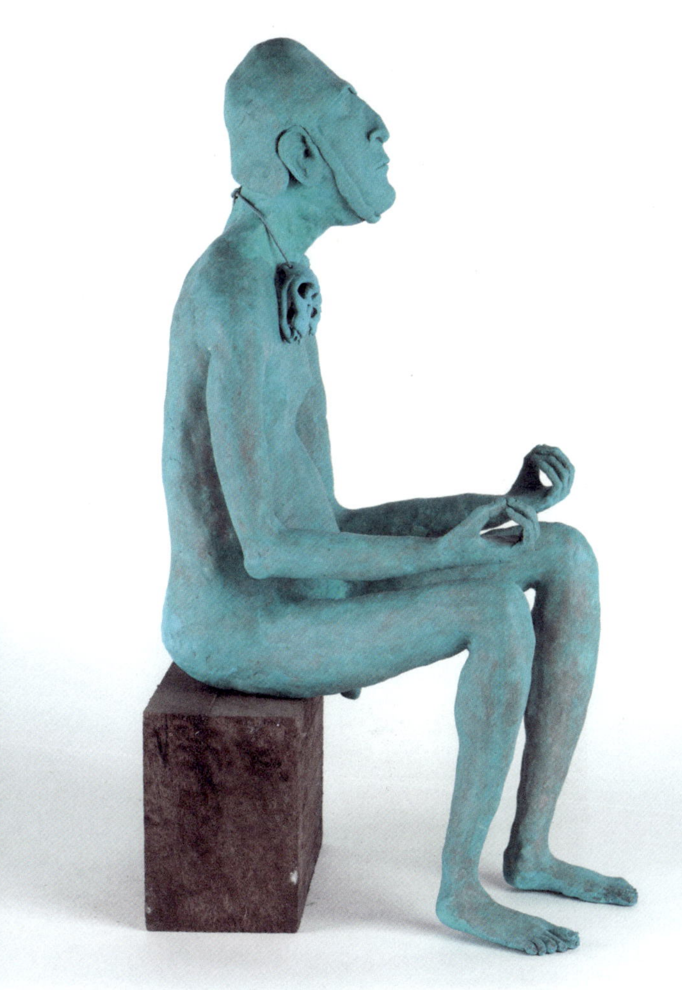

25 a

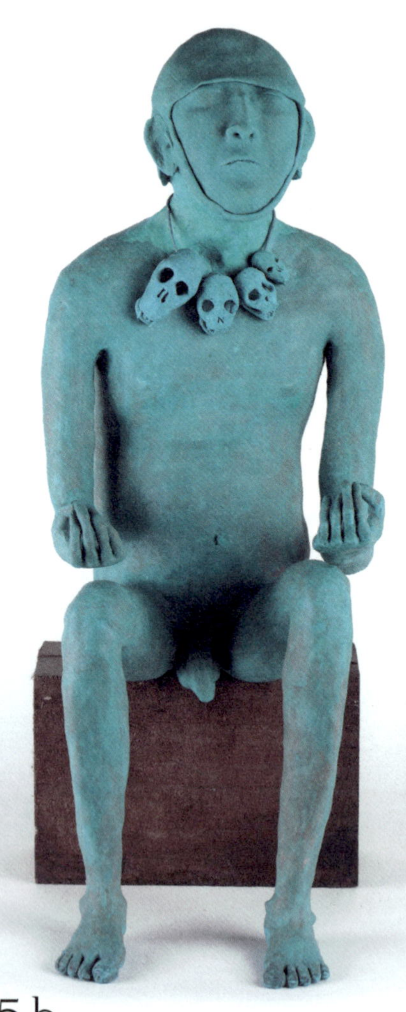

25 b

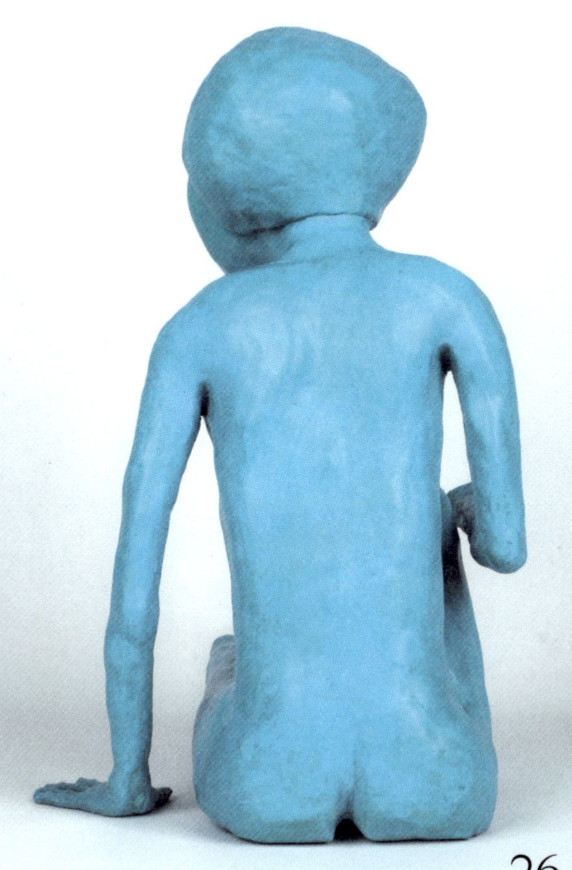

26 a

26 b

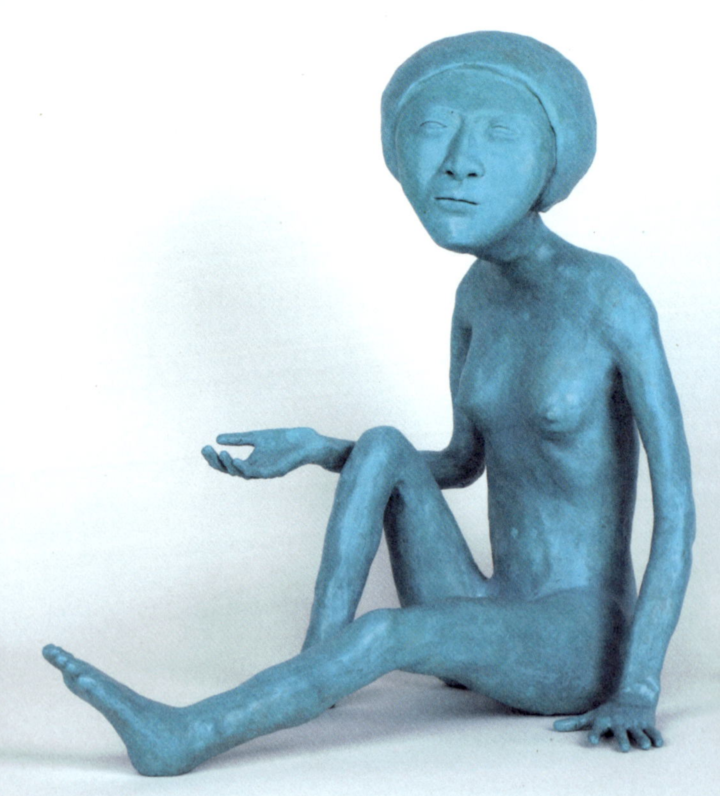

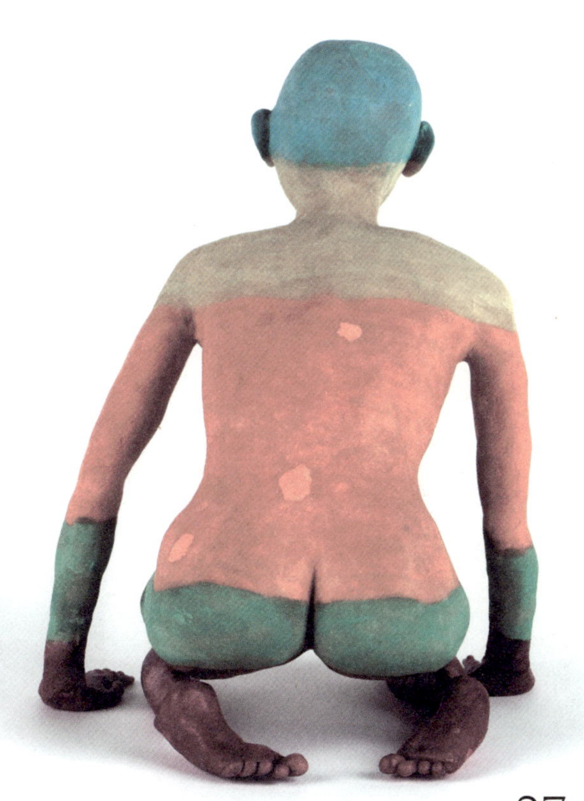

27 a

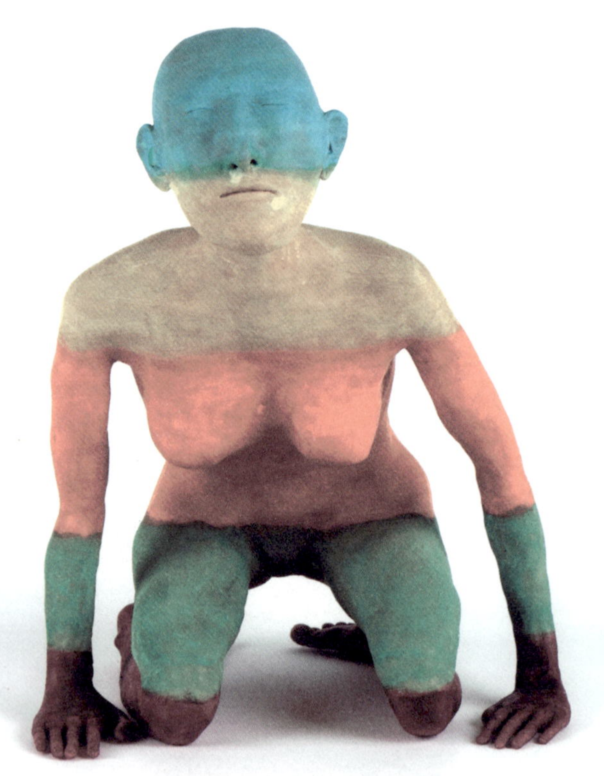

27 b

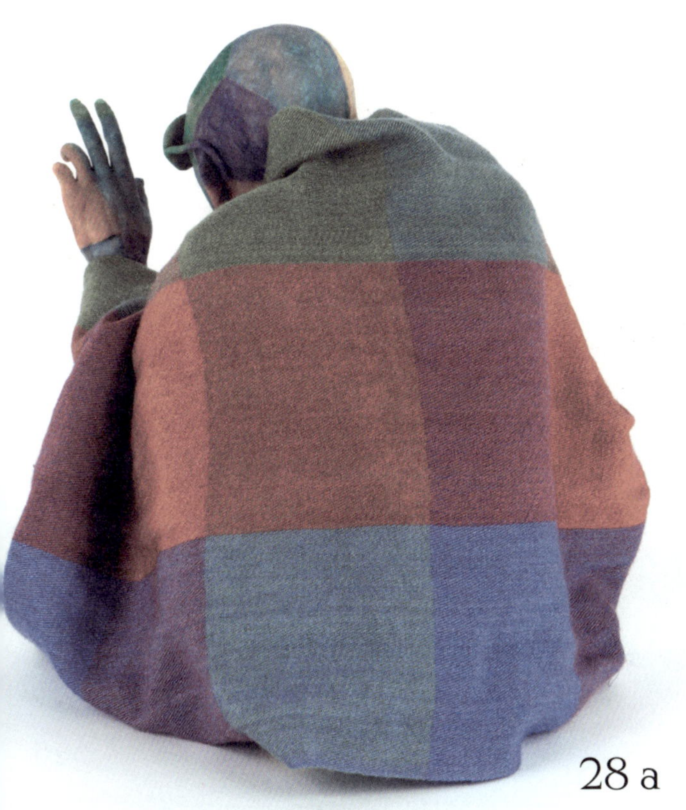

28 a

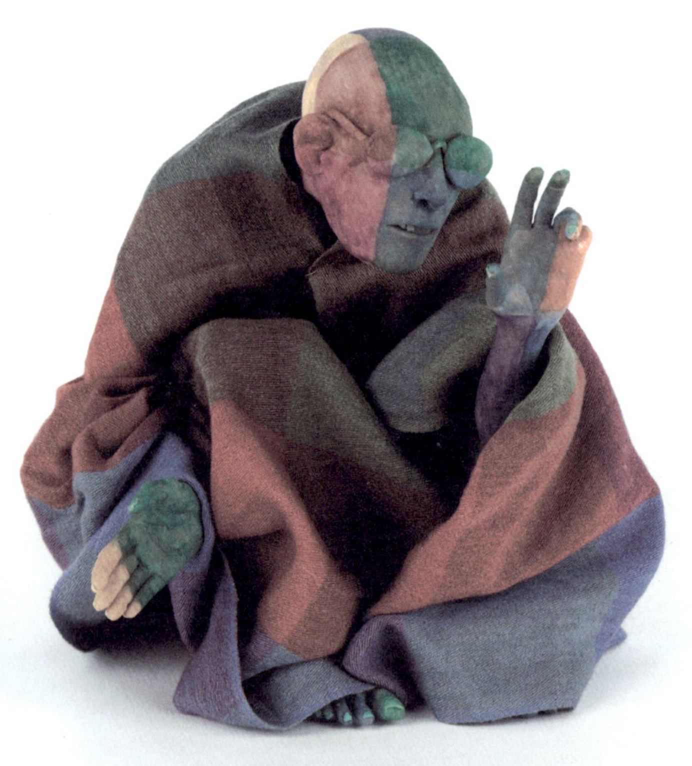

28 b

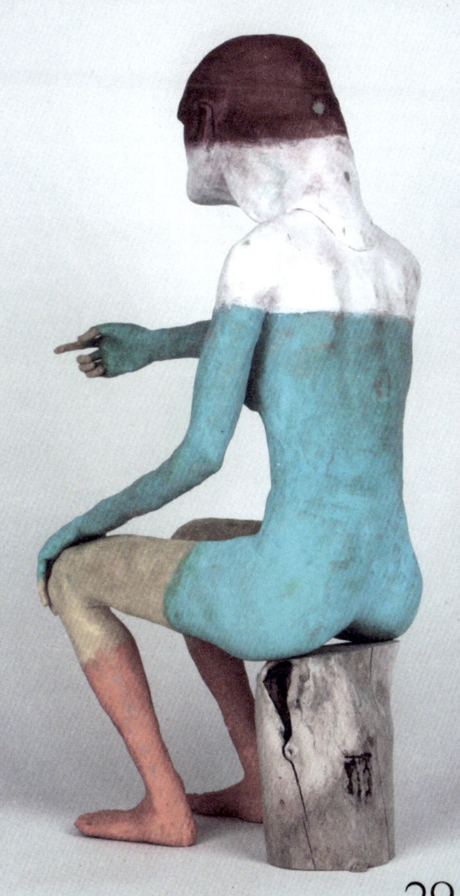

29 a

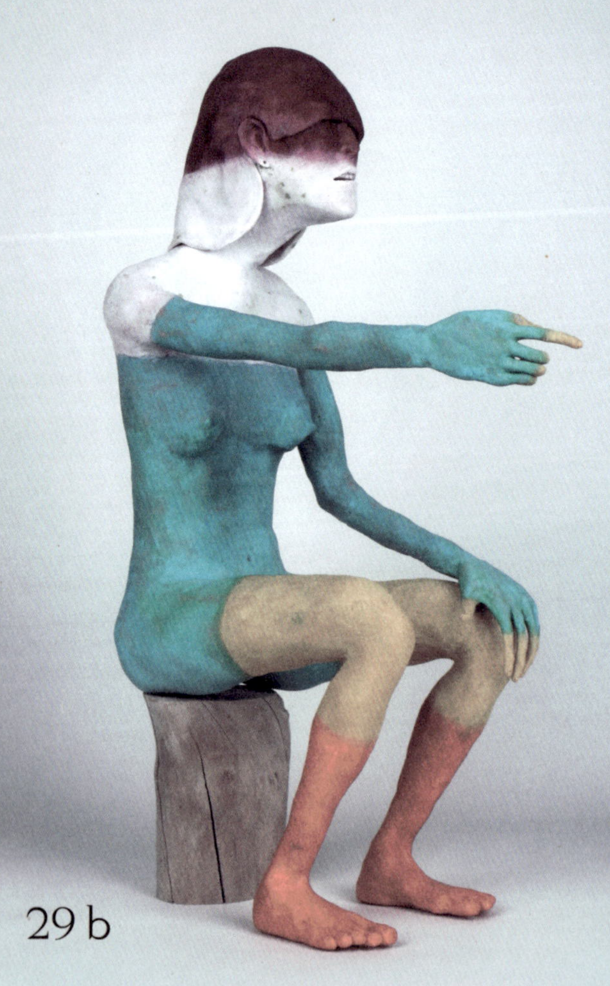

29 b

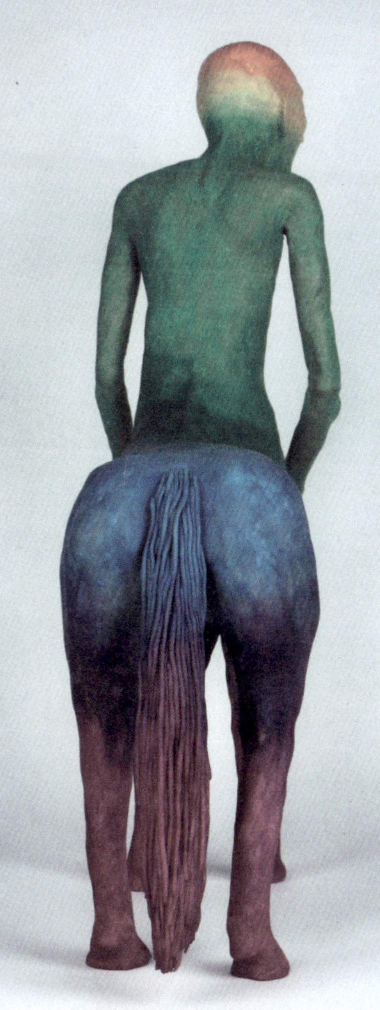

30 a

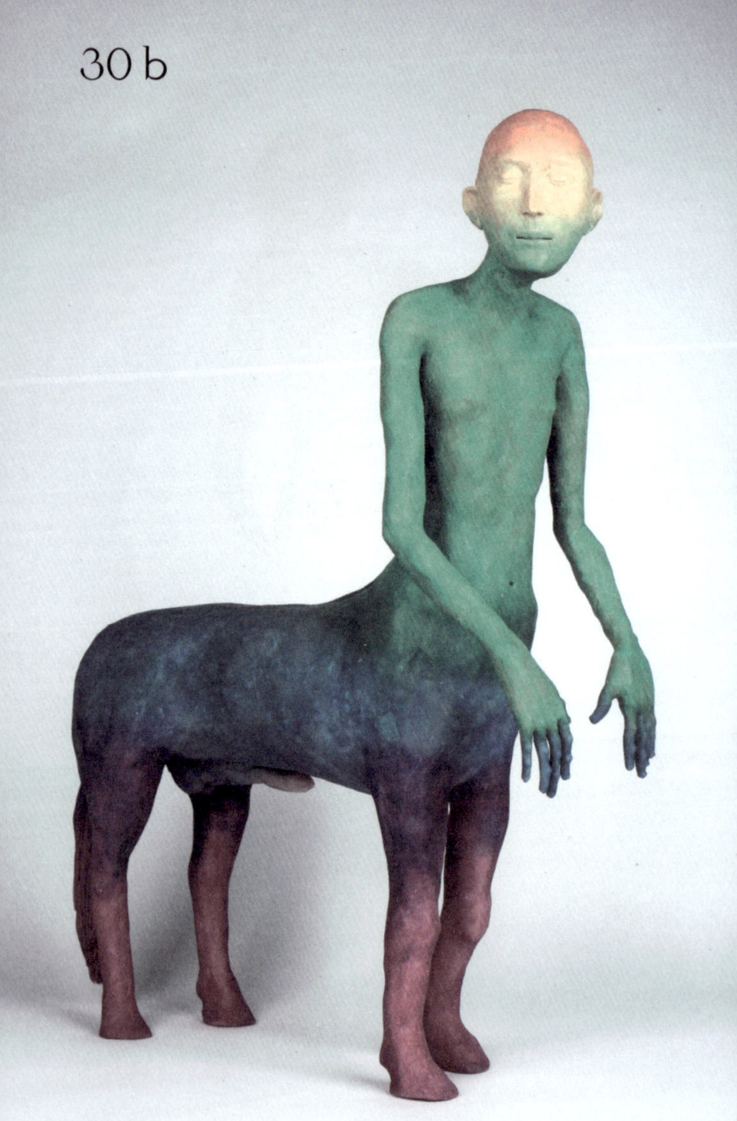

30 b

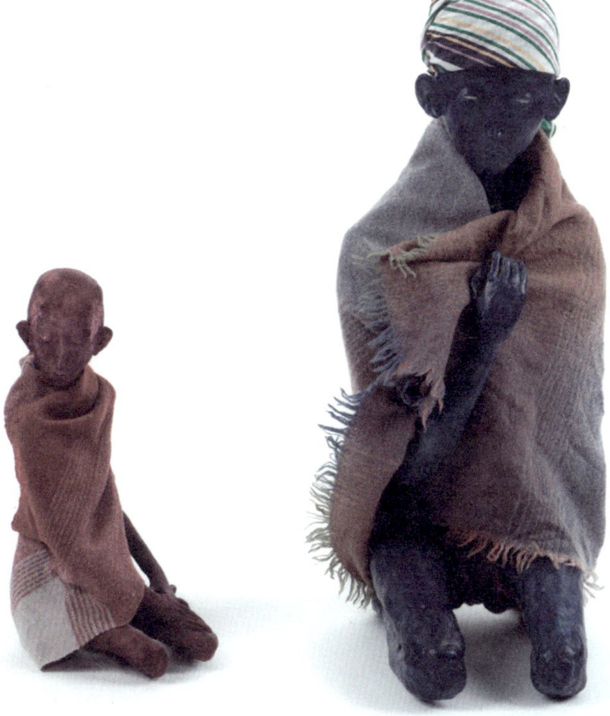

31 a

32 a

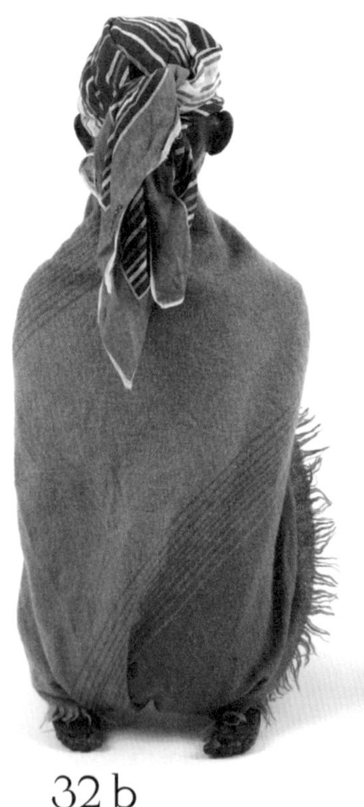

32 b

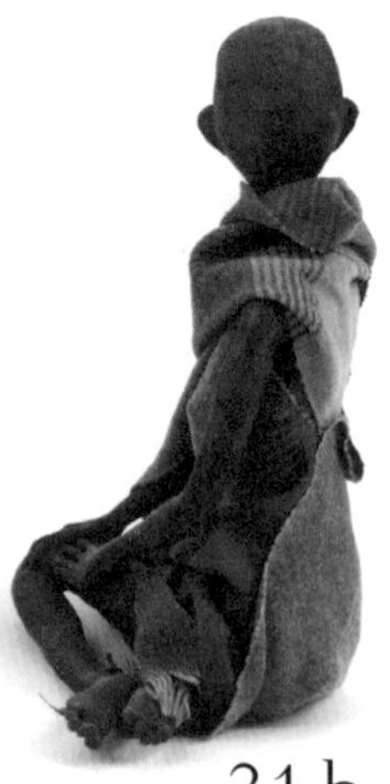

31 b

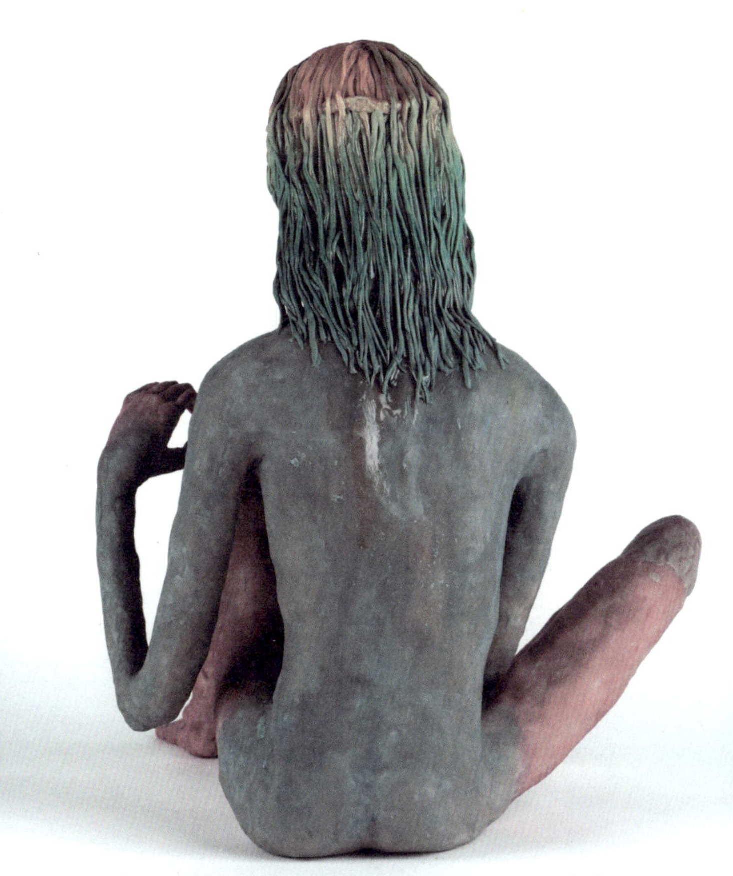

33 a

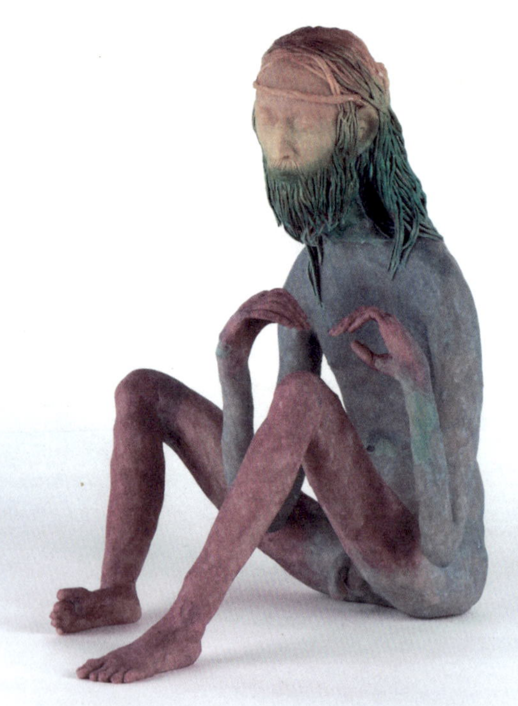

33 a

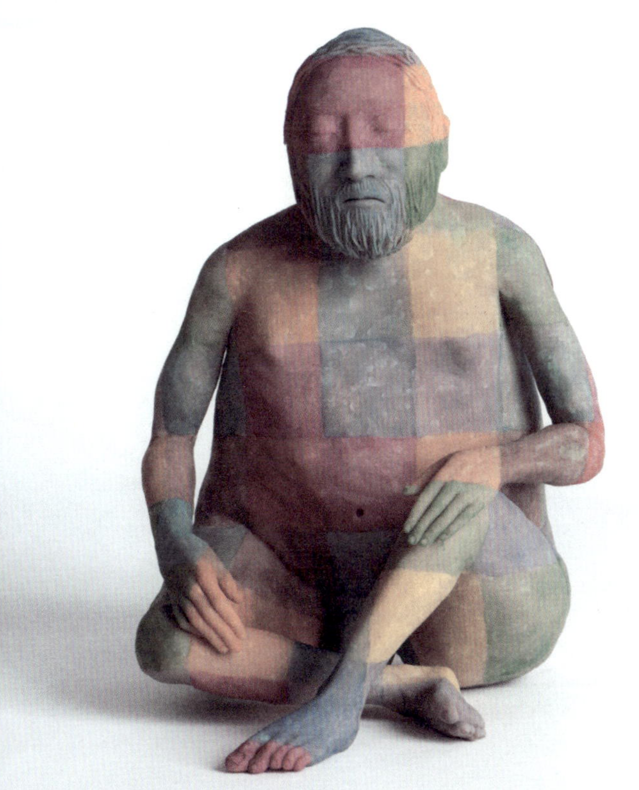

34 a

34 b

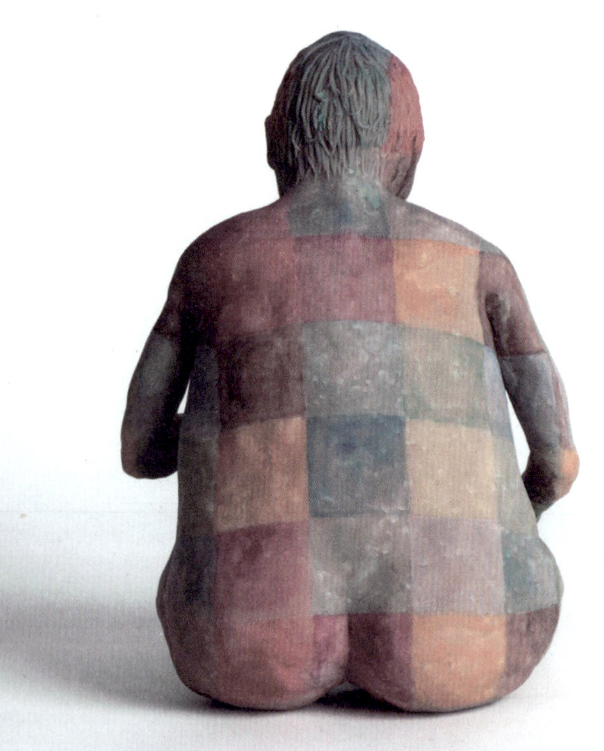

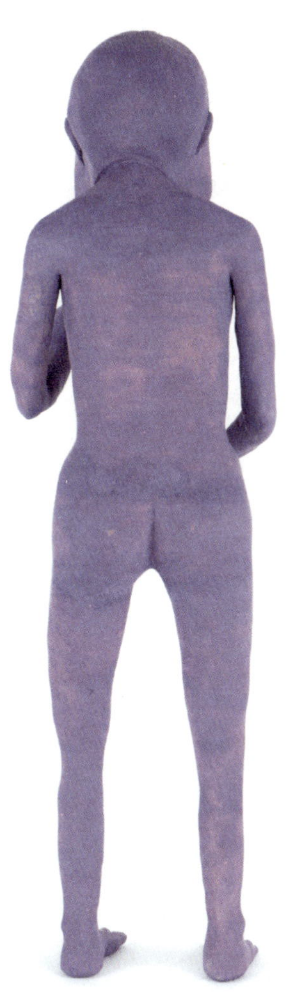

35 a

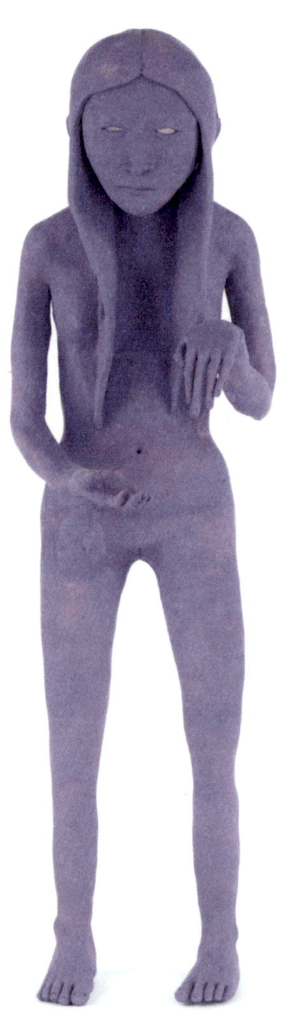

35 b

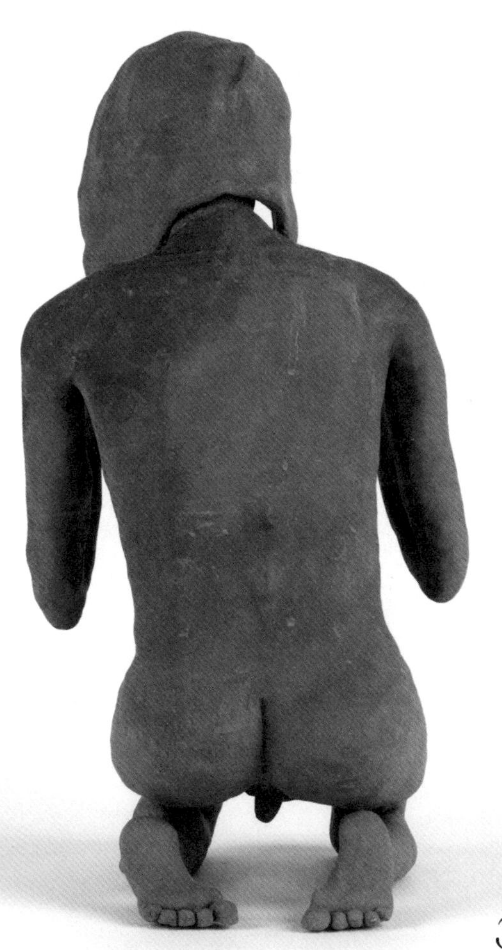

36 a

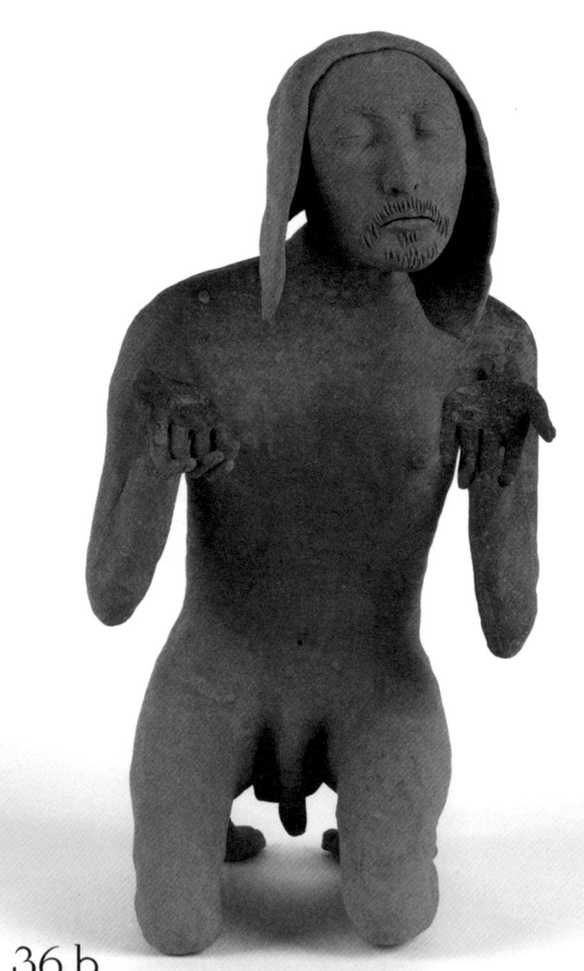

36 b

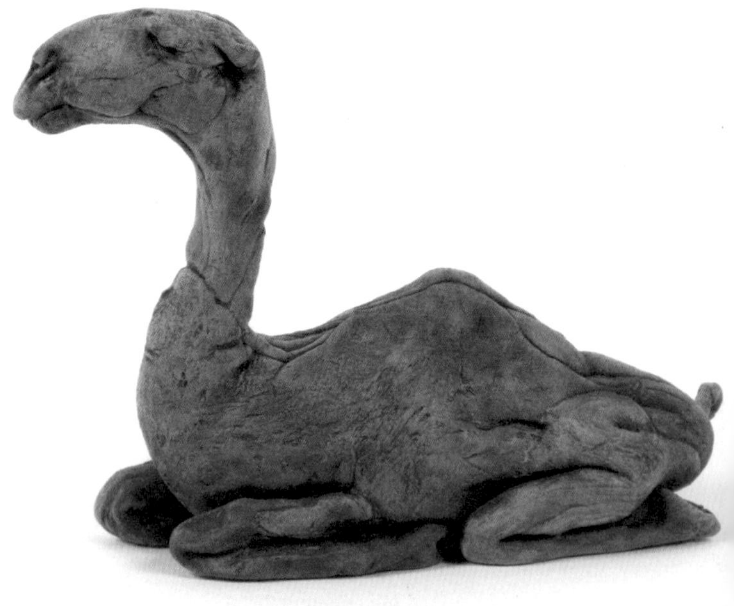

37

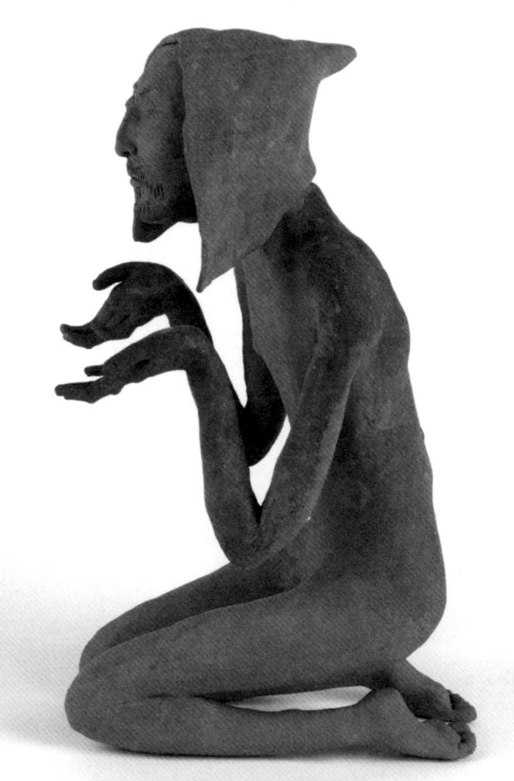

36 c

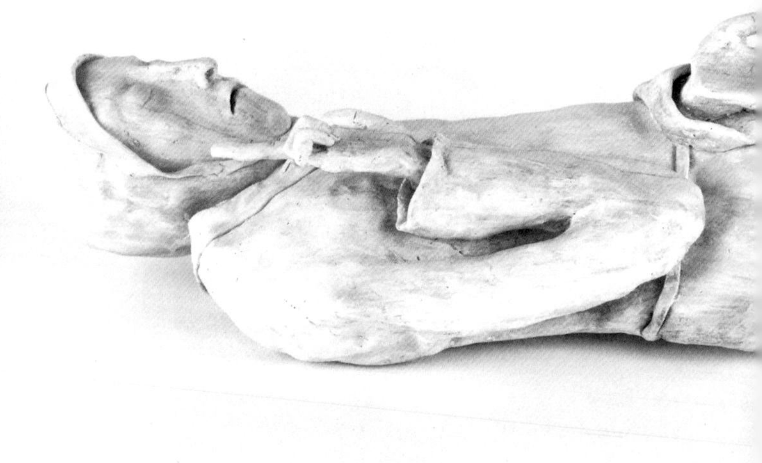

38

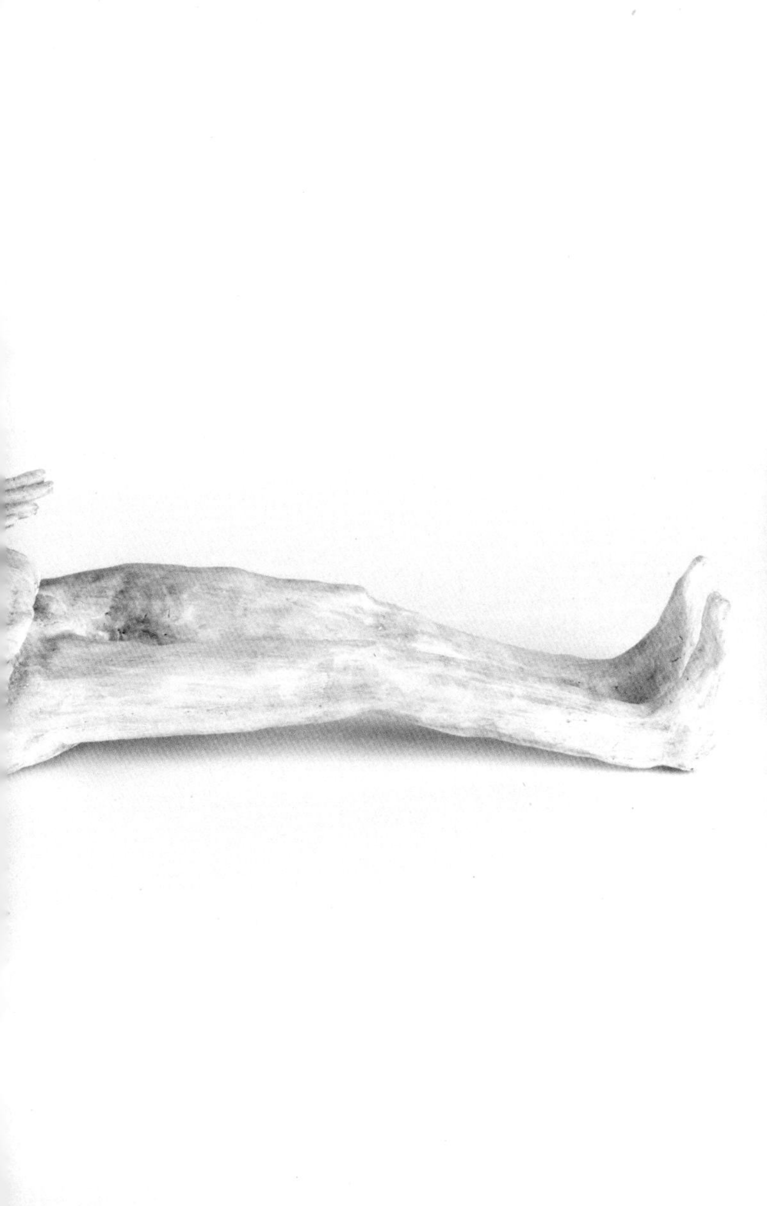

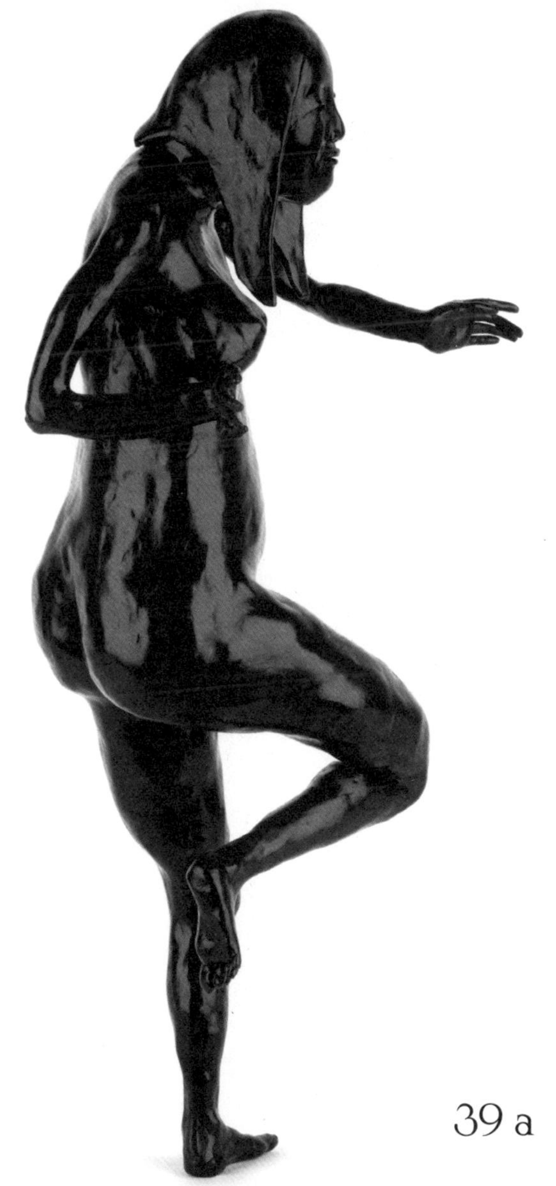

39 a

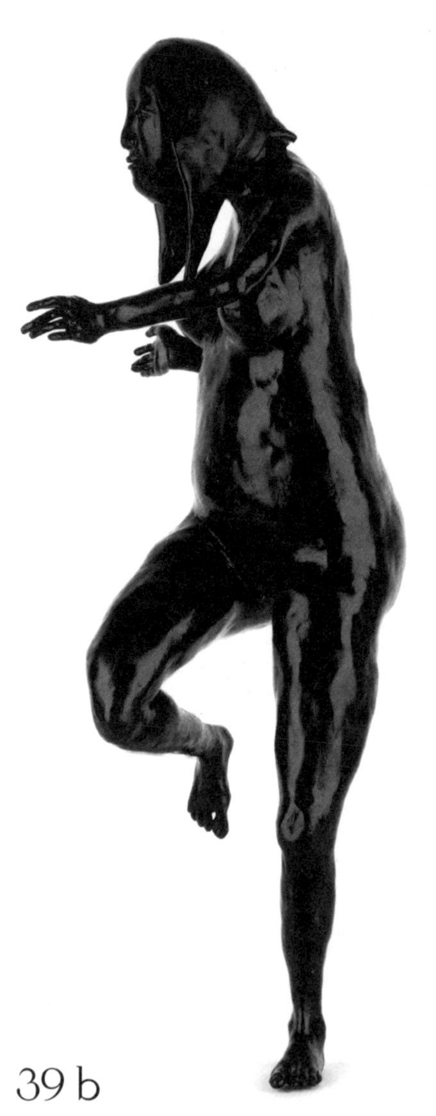

39 b

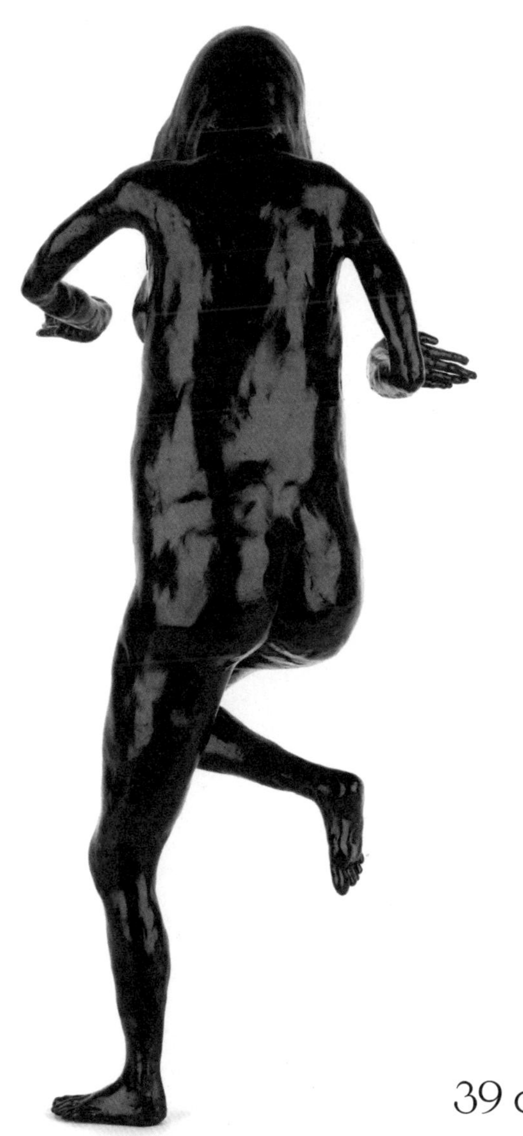

39 c

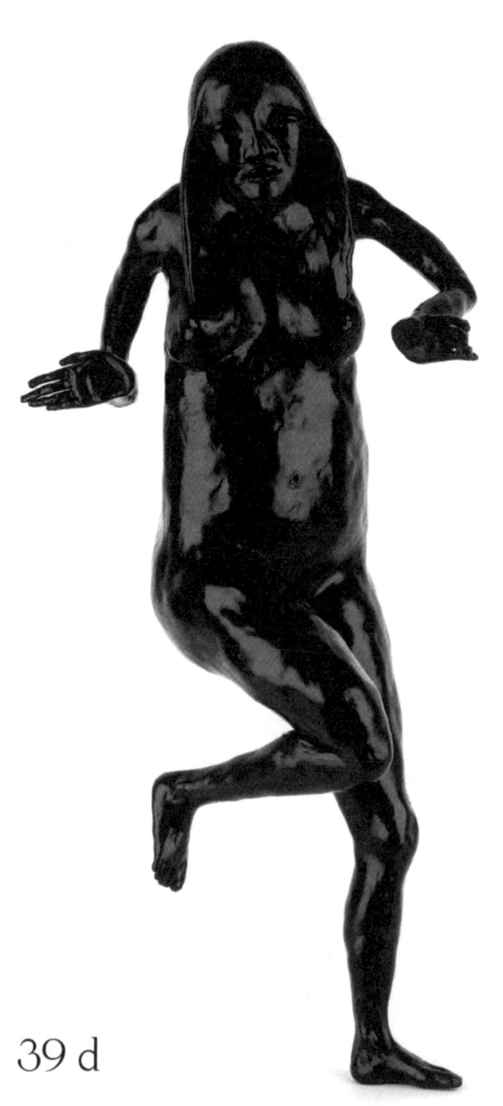

39 d

All the figures are made with modelling material, foil, wire, paint unless otherwise stated. All dimensions are in cm in this order: height x width x depth

1
The Thinker
{2007}
(from Unmoving)
... and wood
37 x 20 x 25

2
Harlequin {2008}
48.5 x 23 x 11.5

3
Milton {2007}
24.5 x 53 x 23

4
Amelia {2007}
64 x 17 x 20

5
Orange Pleader {2008}
57.5 x 15.5 x 22.5

6
House Person {2008}
59 x 22 x 15.5

7
Yellow Figure {2007}
32 x 33 x 17

8
Becoming Cold {2008}
36 x 19.5 x 23

9
Geezer in Car {2008}
40 x 33 x 38

10
Ibis Is The Only Animal
{2008}
24.5 x 16 x 12.5

11
Aphid {2008}
33.5 x 33 x 20.5

12
Werner {2008}
... and wood ·
44 x 17.5 x 17

13
Green Figure {2007}
... on found cabinet
66 x 20 x 22

14
The Gentleman
{2008}
54.5 x 21.5 x 20

15
Sith Lord Thulsa Doom
Bottle {2008}
... and glass
31 x 32 x 32

16
Bone Dancer {2009}
... and cloth
54 x 33 x 14.5

17
Yellow Dancer {2009}
... and cloth
49 x 39.5 x 24.5

18
Winker {2007}
... and wood
44 x 23 x 21.5

19
Warrior {2008}
40.5 x 23.5 x 18.5

20
Maki {2008}
62 x 17 x 21

21
Heepy {2008}
... and cloth
32 x 25 x 20